Preface

Oxfam is a voluntary overseas aid organisation which raises funds from the public and channels them to finance projects of other agencies working overseas. Founded by a group of citizens in Oxford in 1942 as the Oxford Committee for Famine Relief, the organisation financed relief schemes in the early years. Only in the 1960s was attention turned to development; and by the end of the decade, over 70% of Oxfam's assistance was to long-term projects. Though in the 1940s and '50s, aid was given to people in need in Europe, Oxfam's aid programme is now concentrated in Africa, Asia and Latin America ("the Third World").

To supervise the more complex projects in this field and to seek out new avenues for assistance, Oxfam employs nearly fifty staff overseas, together with a small but growing number of specialists (e.g. medical, engineering) and a small professional staff at its headquarters.

Acting on their advice and in consultation with voluntary expert field committees at home, Oxfam draws up general priorities, both in terms of types of aid and in geographical areas. These are constantly under review, reflecting both the needs in particular areas and the existing agencies through whom Oxfam can channel funds, as well as the availability of income for distribution. Brief descriptions of Oxfam's aid in relevant countries have been included in this book. When Oxfam for various reasons has been unable to help, there is no such description.

Oxfam's aid has been running at the £10 million mark in recent years. This is made up of hundreds of individual grants to different projects (many of them in countries not included in this book) ranging in size from £50 to the occasional exceptionally large grant of over £100,000 in an emergency.

Anyone desiring further details of Oxfam's overseas aid programme should write to the Information Department, Oxfam, 274 Banbury Road, Oxford OX2 7DZ.

Introduction

This recipe book sets out to make available to cooks in the United Kingdom some tasty dishes that are made in other continents. We hope you will cook each of them once or twice and then adapt them to your own taste.

Most people in the world never use a recipe book but learn from their relatives and friends. Favourite dishes are handed down from generation to generation.

In order to bring these recipes to you, we have had to write them down, and so we have had to be precise where we should have preferred to be flexible. Since cooking is an art, we hope you will gain confidence as you use ingredients that may now be unfamiliar to you, and come to rely more on your sense of taste and smell than on this book.

Certain principles guided us in the selection of recipes. We tried not to select those that were exploitative of the environment, for example, dishes demanding large quantities of beef. We have preferred to choose recipes where cheaper cuts of meat supplemented vegetable dishes or non-animal sources of protein.

We have, where possible, given priority to dishes showing good dietary practice, for example, fibre-rich foods.

For readers who wish to learn more about diets of people in Third World countries living at subsistence level, we have at Oxfam House diet sheets and some simpler recipes.

Edited by Marieke Clarke

Cover photographs by Geoffrey Priestland

Acknowledgements

We are very grateful to the following people for their encouragement and help with this book: —

Margaret Billett and the Community Education Trust
Gerry Davis
Mildred Masheder
Jacquie Watson of ILEA
Mrs. M. Cay, formerly of the Home Economics Teachers' Centre, Polytechnic of the South Bank
Thelma Lewis of Caribbean Workshop
Michelle Bovey and Christine Traxon
Dr Geoffrey Masefield
Ralph Russell
Gawher Rizvi
Ghita Vyas
Saral Gujral

The following people have most generously helped by letting us use recipes: —

Claudia Roden, for her personal interest in this book
Kenneth Lo and Penguin Books Ltd.
Leonie Acquah
Shirley Ardener
Laura Beauregard Rodriguez de la Serna
Sandra Burman
Cyprus High Commission
Mrs. K. Davis
Pat Diskett
Marijke Drayer-Poortman
Angela Greenwood and C.I.I.R.
Barbara Harrell-Bond
India House
Janet McCrae
Neczam, Zambia
Peckham Publishing Project
S. Puvanachandran
Quaker Peace and Service
Pam Ranasinghe
Heather Redshaw
Rosemary Ridd
Scientific Research Council of Jamaica
Nicki Sissons
Peter Sketchley
Jane Skinner
Elizabeth Stamp
Gene Teo
Lynn Teskey
Sally Thomas
Velma
Suzanne Williams
Melodie Winch
Alberta Wright
Rebecca Young

Contents

	Electric		Gas Mark
	(°F)	(°C)	
Very slow oven	250 - 275	120 - 140	¼ - ½
Slow	300 - 325	150 - 160	1 - 2
Moderate	350 - 375	180 - 190	3 - 5
Moderately hot	375 - 400	190 - 200	5 - 6
Hot	400 - 425	200 - 220	6 - 7
Very hot	450 - 475	230 - 250	8 - 9

1 cup = about 3 oz or 84 grams.

List of recipes by country

ALGERIA
Chervah
Algerian meat balls

BOLIVIA
Baked corn

BRAZIL
Bacalhau com batatas
Feijoada
Biriba
Brigadeiros

BURMA
Egg curry
Mowndi

CARIBBEAN
How to cook some Caribbean vegetables
Dumplings
Salt fish and cabbage

Cuba
Arroz con frijoles
Avocado and pineapple salad

Haiti
Cheese stuffed aubergines

Jamaica
Dukunoo
Rice and peas
Chicken
Escoveitched fish
Pineapple fool

CENTRAL AMERICA

Guatemala
Fresh corn soup
Baked bananas

Honduras
Bean casserole
Maize tortillas

Nicaragua
Tortilla rollups
Pork and fruit

CHILE
Maize pie
Empañadas

CHINA
Sliced beef with green peppers
Minced spiced beef with bean curd
Spiced spare ribs
Chicken in tin foil
Shrimps or prawns in hot garlic sauce
Minced pork balls with cabbage
Eggplant in hot garlic sauce

Stirfried quick braised double winter
Toffee apples and bananas
Szechuan date pancakes

COLOMBIA
Sopa de ajiaco de papas

CYPRUS
Youvarlacia soup
Aubergine moussaka
Village salad

EGYPT
Meat with courgettes and chickpeas

INDIAN SUB-CONTINENT

Vegetarian dishes
Channa dal
Pea and cashew nut stew
Red lentils and tomato stew
Bhurta

Non-vegetarian dishes
Biryani
Chicken kurma
Nargisi kofta
Royal chops
Lamb curry

Snacks and side dishes
Samosas
Pakoras
Mint or coriander leaf chutney
Tomato chutney
Puris
Raita

INDONESIA
A meat dish
Egg and tomato sambal
Serikaya
Sate kambing
Fish on ginger sauce
Sate ajam
Soto ajam

JORDAN
Labna

KAMPUCHEA
Royal rice

KENYA
Mahamri (Swahili buns)
Grilled fish in coconut

LEBANON
Kofta bil Sania
Fattush
Mudardana

MALAYSIA
Curry lunch
Pork sweet and sour

2

MEXICO
Orange candy

Ceviche

Mexican bread pudding

MOROCCO
Vegetable couscous
Orange salad
Orange and radish salad

MOZAMBIQUE
Avocado salad
Barbecued chicken

NEPAL
Aluko chop
Paneu

PACIFIC ISLANDS
Kokoda
Fish baked in soy sauce and ginger

PERU
Shrimp chowder
Anticuchos
Arroz tapado
Lima beans and bacon
Papas à la Huancaina

SOMALIA
Spiced tea
Seafood stew

SOUTH AFRICA
Bobotie
Onion salad
Cape kedgeree
Bouba
Pumpkin fritters
Pickled fish

SRI LANKA
Soojee halwa
Onion sambol
Fish curry

SUDAN
Ful-Sudani
Salata ma jibna

TANZANIA
Coconut bean soup
Spinach with groundnuts
Chicken curry
Avocado apricot jelly
Fish croquettes
Maize and spinach mix

TUNISIA
Chakchouka
Salata Meshwiya

TURKEY
Çilbir
Haricot bean salad

VIETNAM
Rolls without meat
Rice with peanuts and coconut
Vietnamese egg crêpes

WEST AFRICA
Abala: savory rice pudding
Mango banana sundae
Joloff rice
Pineapple nut bread
Groundnut stew

ZAIRE
Meat and bacon dish
Rissoles of peanuts and potatoes

ZAMBIA
Polenta pie

ZIMBABWE
Roast pumpkin
Passionfruit cream
Bean soup
Green mealie fritters

Algeria

Population	18.9 million
Area	2,382,000 square km.
	919,000 square miles
Arable land	7,509,000 hectares
	18,554,000 acres
Life expectation	1960, 47 years; 1980, 56 years
Infant mortality	1960, 165 deaths
	1980, 118 deaths
Population increase rate	3.2%
Labour force in agriculture	48%
Urbanisation	1960, 30%; 1980, 44%
Big city	Algiers, the capital, 1.7mn.
Food index	80%
Daily calorie supply per head	2372 calories, 97%
Basic food crops	Barley, wheat
Major exports	Oil and gas
Income per head	£795
Adult literacy	35%
Climate	Temperate on the coast, varying to hot and dry in the south

Algeria became independent in 1962 after a war of independence lasting six years. Since then, the ruling National Liberation Front has encouraged industrialisation rather than agriculture, using the country's plentiful supplies of oil and natural gas.

North Africa was a granary of the Roman Empire, but now imports massive amounts of food. In 1981, Algeria imported more cereals than she grew.
But people probably eat better than in the late 1960s, and food prices are subsidised.

Much of the land is becoming less fertile because grain is grown on marginal land, there are too many farm animals on too little land and because wood is used for fuel.

Oxfam-supported projects in Algeria
In 1980/81 Oxfam gave several grants to Algeria, most notably £20,000 in supplies and equipment for refugees from the Western Sahara, and £49,075 for earthquake victims.

Chervah (Soup)

Ingredients

1 lb (450 grms) neck of mutton
½ lb (225 grms) tomatoes
¾ lb (336 grms) onions, sliced
Dessertspoon chopped mint
Salt
½ teaspoon red pepper
1 quart water (about 1 litre)
¼ lb (112 grms) vermicelli (optional)
Soya bean oil

Method

1. Brown the onions in the oil and then remove.
2. Put into a stewpan the neck of mutton, the tomatoes, the onions, the mint.
3. Season these ingredients with plenty of salt and the red pepper.
4. Add the water and bring to the boil. Then simmer for 2-2½ hours.
5. Warm a deep tureen.
6. Remove the bones from the soup and serve the soup in the tureen.
7. Cook the vermicelli with the soup or separately. Shake the vermicelli into the soup when it is served.

Source: Quaker Peace and Service

Algerian meatballs

Ingredients

2 slices dry bread
¼ pint of milk
1lb (450 grms) beef or lamb, minced
1 large onion, finely chopped
¼ level teaspoon dried dill
4 tablespoons chopped fresh parsley
or 2 tablespoons dried parsley
½ level teaspoon dried mint or 1 level teaspoon chopped fresh mint
1 egg, lightly beaten
¾ level teaspoon salt
¼ level teaspoon pepper
Soya bean oil or fat for deep frying

Makes 18-24 appetisers

Method

1. Soak bread in milk until soft; squeeze out excess milk.
2. To the bread add all ingredients except the fat for frying.
3. Mix these ingredients very thoroughly; if the mixture is too thick to shape easily, add some of the milk in which the bread was soaked.
4. Roll mixture into one inch balls. (3 cm)
5. Fry the balls a few at a time in deep fat at 370°F (180°C) until balls are golden brown.
6. Remove from fat, drain and serve.

Source: 'Cookbook of the United Nations' by Barbara Kraus

Bolivia

Bolivia is one of the very few Latin American countries to have had a far-reaching revolution and land reform. After the revolution of 1952, estate lands were distributed to tenant farmers and labourers who had previously worked them. But many of the new farms were too small to support a family. Most of the new farmers had had no training in modern techniques and they had poor tools.

The agrarian revolution did not provide the peasants with much of the necessary infra-structure of development: neither roads nor education, credit facilities nor extension services.

An Oxfam-supported project

CIPCA is one of the organisations which is trying to help the peasant farmers by providing technical assistance and cheap inputs such as fertiliser. CIPCA have run educational programmes and encouraged the organisation of co-operatives for production and marketing.

With the Potato Producers' Association, which is made up of 70 local co-operatives, CIPCA ran an educational programme in the local language using short courses, publications and radio programmes. These helped the people become more aware of the overall problems of Bolivian rural society.

An Oxfam staff member wrote in April 1979: "One of the abiding memories of any trip to the CIPCA offices is the continual flow of peasants passing through the recording studios, doing interviews or preparing reports on conditions and events in their home communities for general transmission".

After the coup d'état of July 1980, CIPCA was closed down. Two offices were raided by para-military forces and much of the contents destroyed. Since then it has been possible to renew some of the work.

Population	5.6 million
Area	1,099,000 sq. km.
	424,000 sq. miles
Arable land	3,370,000 hectares
	8,327,000 acres
Life expectation	1960, 43 years; 1980, 50 years
Infant mortality	1960, 167 deaths
	1980, 131 deaths
Population increase rate	2.5%
Labour force in agriculture	49%
Urbanisation	1960, 24%; 1980, 33%
Big city	La Paz, the capital, 729,000
Food index	106%
Daily calorie supply per head	1974 calories, 87%
Basic food crops	Potatoes, maize, cassava
Major exports	Tin, cocaine
Income per head	£242
Adult literacy	63%
Climate	Tropical below about 1500 metres, and cool above about 3500 metres

Baked corn

Ingredients

11oz (308 grms) tin sweet corn or 5 cobs fresh corn
2 eggs
0.5 oz (14 grms) margarine
1/8 level teaspoon chilli powder
1 clove garlic, crushed or chopped
1 level teaspoon flour
4 oz (112 grms) cheese

2 servings

Method

1. Scrape kernels from uncooked corn, or open tins.
2. Beat eggs and combine with corn in a bowl.
3. Heat margarine, add chilli powder, chopped or crush garlic and flour. Cook for one minute.
4. Combine with corn and egg mixture.
5. Pour half of the mixture into a well-oiled 1 ½ pint (0.85 litre) casserole.
6. Cover with some thin slices of cheese.
7. Pour in rest of corn mixture.
8. Cover with the rest of the cheese.
9. Cook for three quarters of an hour in a very moderate oven 350°F. Mark 3.

Source: This recipe appeared in a slightly different form in 'The Cookbook of the United Nations' by Barbara Kraus.

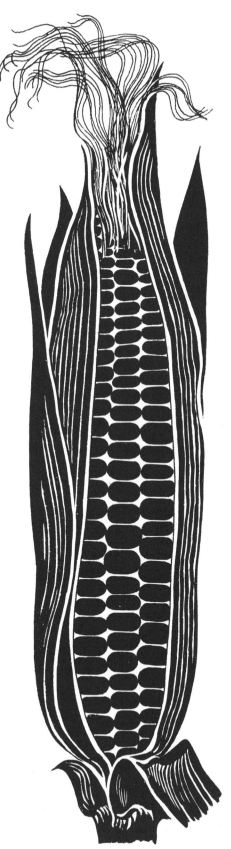

7

Brazil

Population	118.7 million
Area	8,512,000 sq. km or 3,286,000 sq. miles
Arable land	61,950,000 hectares 153,078,000 acres
Life expectation	1960, 55 years; 1980, 63 years
Infant mortality	1960, 118 deaths; 1980, 77 deaths
Population increase rate	2.2%
Labour force in agriculture	37.4%
Urbanisation	1960, 46%; 1980, 68%
Big cities	Brasilia, the capital, 1.2 mn. Sao Paulo, 8.5 mn. Rio de Janeiro, 5.1 mn.
Food index	117%
Daily calorie supply per head	2562 calories, 111 %
Basic food crops	Wheat, rice, maize, cassava
Major exports	Soya products, transport goods, coffee, iron ore, machinery
Income per head	£872
Adult literacy	76%
Climate	Mainly tropical and subtropical. Mild on the southern coast and on the higher land.

Brazil is lavishly endowed with natural resources. It has more arable land than the whole of Europe, nearly 2 million square miles of forest, the world's largest hydro-electric power potential and enormous mineral deposits.

But the country is a typical example of polarised development: a modern capital-intensive, foreign-dominated prosperous sector has grown at the expense of a traditional sector which includes three-quarters of the people.

Inland north-eastern Brazil, for example, is one of the world's most destitute regions where more than 2 million landless families scrape a living from a few months of seasonal agricultural work. Life expectation in the north of Brazil is several years lower than in the south.

In 1982 Brazil could no longer pay the interest on its foreign loans, and the international banking fraternity had to bale it out.

An Oxfam-supported project

An Oxfam-supported project, MOC is a community development project working in north-east Brazil. The staff of 14 work with about 70 peasant and poor urban communities in and around a market town. Many of the rural people have to farm land which is not theirs, and rich landowners reap much of the benefit of their work. Some rural people grow pineapples for 6-8 months a year and are then unemployed.

MOC staff try to help these people to discuss and reflect on the socio-economic and political situation which produces the poverty in which they live. MOC staff hope that through this process the poor people will seek ways of resolving their situation through community action and community solutions.

MOC staff also run an agricultural programme, promoting training sessions, community vegetable gardens, storage experiments etc.

8

Bacalhau com batatas
(Cod and potatoes)

Ingredients
1 lb. (450 grms) dry or smoked cod
3 eggs
1 large green pepper
2 lbs (900 grms) potatoes
½ lb. (225 grms) fresh or tinned tomatoes
1 clove garlic (optional)
Parsley and other herbs such as rosemary
Tin of tomato purée
Olives (optional)

5 servings

Method
1. If you are using dried cod, soak it for about 12 hours in cold water, renewing the water every 2 hours.
2. Hard boil, peel and slice 3 eggs; peel and boil the potatoes.
3. Fry onions, pepper, garlic and tomatoes.
4. Boil the fish until lightly cooked, then flake and remove bones.
5. Slice the potatoes and put them in layers alternating with the fish and the vegetables in an oven-proof dish.
6. Top them with the sliced eggs and olives and pour over them a tomato sauce made from the purée and herbs.
7. Put the dish in a moderate oven until the fish is cooked.

Feijoada (Black beans and meat)

(Pronounced Fezh-wa-da)
The basic ingredient of Feijoada is black beans (sometimes called "Red wonder beans" or Lima beans). These are mixed with various kinds of sausage and meat to produce a very rich, tasty dish. Almost any meat can be used, but especially pork.
Quantities are not very important; poorer people in Brazil eat beans and rice with no meat and this is also very tasty.

Ingredients
2 cups of black beans
½ lb. (225 grms) bacon
½ lb. (225 grms) smoked sausage
1 pig's foot
Any other bits of meat (e.g. garlic sausage, fresh sausage, tongue, etc.)
2 large onions
1 clove garlic
Seasoning

8 servings

Method
1. Soak the beans overnight.
2. Allow 3 or 4 hours to boil them, or less if you use a pressure cooker. Do not add salt until the beans are soft.
3. Fry onions until lightly browned with any fresh meat.
4. Add to beans and allow to cook for at least one hour.

Biriba : Doce de Coco
(Coconut dessert)

Ingredients
1 grated coconut
1 tin sweetened condensed milk
4 eggs
1 tablespoon butter or margarine
1 cup sugar
1 teaspoon vanilla

Method
1. Put all the ingredients into a thick-bottomed saucepan.
2. Cook slowly on a low heat, stirring continuously.
3. The dish is ready when you can clearly see the bottom of the saucepan as you are stirring.

Source: Melodie Winch

Brigadeiros

Ingredients
1 tin of condensed milk
Equal measure of milk
1 dessertspoon butter
2 dessertspoons chocolate powder
2 egg yolks

Method
1. Mix all the ingredients and cook until the mixture comes away from the bottom of the pan.
2. Pour the mixture onto a plate.
3. While the mixture is still warm, make little balls and roll them in chocolate wotsits or hundreds and thousands.

Source: Suzanne Williams

Population	34.8 million
Area	677,000 sq. km
	261,000 sq. miles
Arable land	10,023,000 hectares
	24,766,000 acres
Life expectation	1960, 44 years; 1980, 54 years
Infant mortality	1960, 158 deaths;
	1980, 101 deaths
Population increase rate	2.4%
Labour force in agriculture	51%
Urbanisation	1960, 19%; 1980, 27%
Big cities	Rangoon, the capital; Mandalay
Food index	99%
Daily calorie supply per head	2286 calories, 103%
Basic food crops	Rice
Major exports	Rice, teak
Income per head	£72
Adult literacy	70%
Climate	Tropical monsoon

Life is simple in Burma but nobody starves. Land belongs to the state and each farmer is allocated a certain amount. Burma seems to have avoided the social injustices of the Green Revolution.

An Oxfam-supported project in Burma

The Wa hill tribe people in Northern Shan State in Burma are mainly farmers inhabiting remote and impoverished mountainous territory bordering China. They are the victims of chronic hostilities between a disaffected minority of Communists trying to set up an autonomous state and Burmese government forces. They are oppressed by both sides and young men are dragooned into serving one side or the other in a struggle with which they do not identify.

To escape this plight they have been fleeing in considerable numbers to the area around Lashio. The Roman Catholic prefect apostolic there has been helping in various ways by providing some basic drugs and small amounts of food. Oxfam gave £2,402 to help 150 Wa people set up carpentry and dressmaking workshops and communal farms, for which land was available. 20 buffaloes would be bought, as well as maize, rice and vegetable seeds and bullock carts.

Egg curry

Ingredients

1 lb (450 grms) onions, very finely chopped
3 cloves garlic, crushed
½ level teaspoon ground ginger
4 tablespoons oil
1 level teaspoon salt
½ level teaspoon turmeric
1 level teaspoon paprika
2 small tins tomato concentrate
½ pint or 0.3 litre water
1 level teaspoon soy sauce
6 hardboiled eggs cut in halves lengthwise
Mushrooms (optional) peeled and sliced

6 servings

Method

1. Heat the oil till it is very hot.
2. Add onions, garlic and ginger to the oil and lower heat.
3. Cook these ingredients until onions are done but not brown.
4. Stir in salt, turmeric and paprika.
5. Gradually add tomato concentrate mixed with water.
6. Bring to the boil and add soy sauce and egg halves.
7. Lower heat and cook until sauce and oil appear to separate and egg whites are tinged with the colour of the sauce.

NB:
1. If mushrooms are added just after the spices, the dish is even more tasty.
2. You are recommended to eat boiled rice with this dish, but Indian wheaten pancakes such as puris are even more delicious. Raita makes a perfect accompaniment to the dish. For both recipes see Indian sub-continent section (Editor).

Source: 'The Cookbook of the United Nations' by Barbara Kraus.

Mowndi

(Noodles with chicken curry and soup)

Ingredients

1 cup oil
2 medium onions, thinly sliced
1 medium sized chicken
6 tablespoons fish sauce
2 large onions, minced
6 large cloves garlic, minced, plus one clove crushed
1 teaspoon grated fresh ginger plus 2 thin slices ginger
1 teaspoon turmeric
5½ cups water
4 small onions, chopped
1-2 pkts. noodles, according to size of packet. Almost any kind of noodle would be suitable except the thin, vermicelli type
2 lemons cut into wedges
1 onion thinly sliced
½ cup pan-roasted chick-pea flour (besan)
powdered chillies
fish sauce

4 servings

Method

1. Fry the two thinly-sliced onions in oil over low flame, stirring occasionally, until golden brown.
2. Drain, spread onions on absorbent paper to become cool and crisp.
3. Set oil aside.
4. Quarter chicken and boil in 4 cups water with 4 tablespoons fish sauce until meat is half-cooked.
5. Strain broth, shred chicken and set aside.
6. Take ¼ cup of the oil in which onions were fried and sauté minced onions, minced garlic and grated ginger, adding turmeric.
7. When the mixture starts to redden, add 2 tablespoons fish sauce, the shredded chicken and 1½ cups of water.
8. Cook until chicken is tender and oil rises to the surface of the thick curry.
9. Add salt to taste.
10. In the meantime, boil the chicken stock with the crushed garlic and sliced ginger.
11. Add salt and pepper to taste; garnish with chopped onions.

To serve:

1. Place boiled noodles, curry and accompaniments including the fried onions and the remaining oil in which they were fried on table for guests to serve themselves.
2. Soup should be served at the same time in small bowls placed at the side of the dinner plates. Chinese bowls with their own matching spoons are most suitable.
3. Add a tablespoon of curry to each portion of noodles, a teaspoon of chick-pea flour, a teaspoon of the remaining onion-oil and the other accompaniments to taste.
4. Mix well. The noodles should be moist but not watery.

Aung San Suu Kyi

CARIBBEAN
Cuba
Haiti
Jamaica

How to cook some Caribbean vegetables

Yams with sweet potatoes

Peel and wash. Cook in same way as potatoes. Cooking time usually 20-25 minutes.

Green bananas

1. Slice off about half an inch (1.5 cm) at the top of the banana.
2. With a sharp knife make a slit through the skin lengthwise down one side of the banana. This makes it possible for the skin to be easily removed when it is cooked.
3. Place the banana in a saucepan with enough water to cover it. Add one tablespoon of sunflower oil and salt to taste.
4. Bring to the boil, then reduce the heat and simmer for 20-25 minutes.
5. When the banana is cooked, skin should peel away easily and naturally.

Dumplings

Ingredients

4 oz (112 grms) plain flour
salt to taste
Water

Method

1. Add enough water to flour and salt to make a firm dough.
2. Knead until the dough is smooth.
3. Divide into portions and form into 2 inch (5 cm) round, ¼ inch (0.6 cm) thick dumplings.
4. Boil in water with the vegetables mentioned above.

Community Education Trust

Salt fish and cabbage

Ingredients

1 packet (salt) dried fish
One quarter of a medium savoy cabbage
Black pepper
1 green chilli, chopped (optional)
1 medium onion, sliced
2 tablespoons oil
1 green pepper, sliced
1 large tomato, sliced

Method

1. Soak fish overnight.
2. Drain fish and then bring to the boil in fresh water.
3. Cook for 10 minutes.
4. Drain the fish and then cut it into small pieces.
5. Pick the flesh off the bones.
6. Shred the cabbage.
7. Fry the onions and green pepper (and green chilli if used) for a few minutes in a frying pan.
8. Add the fish pieces, cabbage, tomato, black pepper.
9. Add approximately ¼ pint (one decilitre) cold water.
10. Stir well and steam gently on medium heat until most of the water is evaporated, but sufficient liquid is left to provide a gravy.

   Two rashers of chopped bacon can be added when you fry the onion and green pepper.

Source: Community Education Trust

Cuba

Population	9.7 million
Area	115,000 sq. km. 44,400 sq. miles
Arable land	3,200,000 hectares
	7,907,000 acres
Life expectation	1960, 63 years; 1980, 73 years
Infant mortality	1960, 66 deaths
	1980, 21 deaths
Population increase rate	1.3%
Labour force in agriculture	22%
Urbanisation	1960, 55%; 1980, 65%
Big city	Havana, 1.9 mn.
Food index	105%
Daily calorie supply per head	2720 calories, 118%
Basic food crops	Rice, maize
Major export	Sugar
Income per head	Not known
Adult literacy	About 96%
Climate	Sub-tropical

After the revolution of 1959, the government tried to ensure that ordinary people gained control of the crucial resources (land, seed, water, fertiliser, credit) so that people's basic needs could be met.

In recent years Oxfam has not been asked to help in Cuba.

Haiti

Population	5 million
Area	28,000 sq. km.
	10,800 sq. miles
Arable land	890,000 hectares
	2,199,000 acres
Life expectation	1960, 44 years; 1980, 53 years
Infant mortality	1960, 182 deaths;
	1980, 115 deaths
Population increase rate	1.7%
Labour force in agriculture	65%
Urbanisation	1960, 16%; 1980, 28%
Big city	Port au Prince, the capital
	494,000
Food index	92%
Daily calorie supply per head	2100 calories, 92%
Basic food crops	Maize, sorghum, bananas
Major exports	Coffee, sugar, bauxite
Income per head	£114
Adult literacy	about 23%
Climate	Tropical

Haiti occupies the western third of the island of Hispaniola, the remaining segment belonging to the Dominican Republic. Two-thirds of Haiti is mountainous and agricultural work is carried out almost always by hand. Only 0.4% of agricultural activity accounting for about one-tenth of cultivable land has access to credit and technical assistance. By contrast, nearly half the agricultural activity is concentrated on 10% of arable land and comprises a total of 293,225 small farms.

An Oxfam-supported project in Haiti

Andrew Royer is a farmer in Dominica with 0.5 hectare (1.2 acres) of land on steep terrain, who has evolved a system of intensive organic farming particularly suited to the Caribbean. He can also explain his methods of farming to other people. He had twice visited Haiti, where peasants and animators from Oxfam-supported projects attended his course for a few days. But several projects asked Mr. Royer to do a 1-month course with them so that they could establish their own gardens, get some income and better advise the small farmer groups with whom they work.

The course concentrates on recycling everything in the garden and associating crops to ensure pest control without chemicals. Andrew Royer also encourages people to record the rainfall and to plant accordingly. He stresses that the garden should be first of all for family consumption and then the surplus should be marketed. He stresses the role of women and the importance of nutrition.

The beneficiaries of the Oxfam-supported projects come from communities where women are accustomed to work outside the home, preparing the land and sowing seed; but their most important function is taking goods to market and selling them.

Many of the beneficiary families eat only one meal a day, mainly consisting of starchy vegetables, with hardly any meat and no milk products. The most important crops are coffee, cane sugar and crops to feed the family of the grower.

Drinking water is likely to be from rivers or springs which may be polluted. The animators who were working with these people were young and needed extra practical farming training to advise on alternative techniques. Oxfam paid £3,772 for Mr. Royer to come from Dominica to Haiti and to run courses for animators working with poor Haitian peasants.

Arroz con frijoles

(Rice with black beans)

Ingredients

8 oz (224 grms) black beans or red kidney beans.
1½ pints (0.84 litre) water.
1 large onion, very finely chopped
2 cloves garlic, crushed
1 level teaspoon pepper
1 bay leaf
1 level teaspoon salt
2 cloves
12 oz (336 grms) rice.
¾ pint (0.32 litre) hot water or more to taste
4 oz (112 grms) smoked ham, very finely chopped
¼ pt (0.14 litre) olive oil
6 to 8 servings

Method

1. Wash the beans thoroughly and let them stand overnight in water in a five pint (2.8 litre) saucepan.
2. Throw away the water next day.
3. Boil the beans in different water for 40 minutes adding more water if necessary. (You can also use a pressure cooker which will take less time). Boil till the beans are really tender, but whole.
4. Add half the onion, garlic, green pepper and seasoning, rice and hot water to the beans.
5. Cover and cook for about 40 minutes over low heat stirring the rice once by turning it from bottom to top.
6. Remove from heat when the rice is tender and dry.
7. Add 4 tablespoons oil and allow to stand for 5 minutes.
8. Meanwhile, heat the ham in the remaining oil and when it is half-fried, add remaining onion, garlic, green pepper and seasoning.
9. Fry till brown, and serve over the beans and rice.

Source: Adapted from 'The Cookbook of the United Nations', by Barbara Kraus

Cheese stuffed aubergines

Ingredients

2 aubergines
Water
2 level tablespoons finely chopped onion
¼ oz (7 grms) butter
2 slices stale bread soaked in ¼ pint (1 decilitre) milk and squeezed dry
2 tablespoons condensed cream of chicken soup
Salt and pepper
1 egg lightly beaten
6 level tablespoons grated cheddar cheese (or a little more)
4 heaped tablespoons breadcrumbs
2 cloves garlic)
pinch cardamom)
pinch cinnamon) optional
pinch cummin   )

4 servings

Method

1. Boil aubergines in water until they are soft and drain.
2. Mash them thoroughly.
3. Cook the onion until it is translucent and add the spices.
4. Cook slowly for a short time.
5. Then add the aubergine to the onion and spice mixture and cook for five minutes.
6. Add the bread, chicken soup, salt and pepper and continue cooking for five minutes.
7. Remove from heat.
8. Stir in egg and enough cheese to make the mixture taste cheesy.
9. Pour into a greased casserole, cover with breadcrumbs and bake for 25 minutes in a very moderate oven (350°F. Mark 3).

Source: Adapted from a recipe in 'Cookbook of the United Nations' by Barbara Kraus

Avocado and pineapple salad

Ingredients

1 ripe avocado
4 slices fresh or tinned pineapple
Lettuce leaves

Dressing

6 teaspoons olive oil
2 teaspoons lemon or lime juice
¼ level teaspoon salt

4 servings

Method

1. Chill avocado and pineapple.
2. Remove peel and stone from avocado.
3. Cut fruit into half-inch cubes and mix them together.
4. Make the dressing by combining all ingredients and shaking well.
5. Add dressing to fruit and mix well.
6. Serve on a bed of lettuce.

Source: 'Cookbook of the United Nations' by Barbara Kraus

Jamaica

For over 300 years most of the available flat, fertile land in Jamaica has been used to grow sugarcane. But there is now a world glut of sugar as sugar is also obtained from beet sugar. There has always been a shortage of good farming land on which Jamaicans can grow food crops for their own domestic use.

Nearly a quarter of the labour force has been unemployed in recent years, partly because of the seasonal character of crop cultivation and partly because of the limited farming and industrial opportunities.

Bauxite, the most important export earner and principal industry, employs relatively few people. The tourist industry is vitally important to the economy, because it employs between 15,000 and 20,000 people (according to the season) and is the second most important source of foreign exchange.

An Oxfam-supported project in Jamaica

"Salisbury Plain has all the conditions for good farming — good soil, good rainfall, proximity to markets in the capital, good roads. The land has a stream from which water can be pumped. Many residents of the area earn a living by selling goods, for example eggs and crops in Kingston market. Unfortunately, most youths in the area are educated for export to Kingston. No emphasis has been placed on farming, hence the recession in the job market has had serious consequences for youths who now look towards self-employment through co-operative enterprises." — Project application to Oxfam.

The Salisbury Plain Community Council decided to encourage some young people to come together to form an agricultural co-operative for livestock production and selling vegetables. After a few months there was a group of 12 to 15 people working together for whom Oxfam gave grants totalling £10,201 to secure land, improve it, buy tools, equipment, and assist members of the group for the first six months; and to construct a pig pen as well as a bio-gas plant.

The project is a pilot one. Through it other youth groups may see the possibilities of working the land.

Population	2.2 million
Area	11,000 sq. km. 4,247 sq. miles
Arable land	265,000 hectares, 654,800 acres
Life expectation	1960, 64 years
	1980, 71 years
Infant mortality	1960, 52 deaths;
	1980, 16 deaths
Population increase rate	1.5%
Labour force in agriculture	19%
Urbanisation	1960, 34%; 1980, 41%
Big city	Kingston, the capital, 643,000
Food index	96%
Daily calorie supply per head	2660 calories, 118%
Basic food crops	Bananas, maize, yams, cassava, sweet potatoes, cocoyam
Major exports	Bauxite, alumina, sugar, bananas
Income per head	£442
Adult literacy	about 90%
Climate	Tropical

16

Dukunoo

Ingredients

1 lb (450 grms) sweet potato
1 coconut — to make a cup of milk
1 teaspoon vanilla
¼ teaspoon cinnamon
¼ teaspoon nutmeg
¼ teaspoon ginger powder
¾ lb or about 336 grms sugar
Rather more than a cup of maize flour
¼ lb or about 125 grms butter
1 egg (if you want) with the eye taken out*
¼ lb (or about 125 grms) mixed fruit (if you want)
Some rum (if you want)
A little salt

Method

1. Peel and grate the sweet potato.
2. Grate the coconut and put it in half a cup of warm water.
3. Knead the coconut with your hand until it is soggy.
4. Then squeeze all the juice out into the bowl with your hand, a handful at a time.
5. Leave the squeezed out coconut (called 'the trash') on a plate at the side.
6. Take a sieve and strain the juice into another bowl.
7. Put the trash back in the first bowl with another half cup of warm water and squeeze it and strain it again.
8. Mix the strained juice with the sweet potato.
9. Add the vanilla, spice and sugar.
10. Put in maize flour or flour till the consistency is firm and mix in remaining ingredients (except for salt).
11. Put on water to boil with a little salt.
12. Wrap some small quantities of the dukunoo mixture in banana leaves or aluminium foil and tie firmly.
13. Cook the dukunoo in boiling water for 1½ hours.

Serve hot or cold with a cup of milk.

Note: This recipe originated in West Africa

Source: 'Captain Blackbeard's Beef Creole'

*In the Caribbean, people always take the eye out of eggs before using them for cooking. That takes the raw taste away. The eye is the little white stringy bit and the red spot.

Rice and peas (Red kidney beans)

Ingredients

½ lb (225 grms) peas (red kidney beans or black eye peas)
2 oz (56 grms) coconut cream
1 lb (450 grms) rice, washed
Half a teaspoon thyme
1 clove garlic, crushed
1 small onion, sliced
Salt to taste

3-4 servings

Method

1. Soak red kidney beans, if used, overnight. Throw away the water.
2. Bring the red kidney beans or black eye peas to the boil in 1½ pints (0.75 litres) fresh water with a pinch of bicarbonate of soda added.
3. Cook for at least one hour on medium heat or half an hour in a pressure cooker, until tender. Throw away the water.
4. Add coconut cream and seasonings and bring back to the boil. Add washed rice and simmer gently until rice is cooked and all the water is absorbed.
5. If rice is not completely cooked add a little water to prevent it sticking.

NB It is most important to check that the red kidney beans are thoroughly cooked as they can be harmful if they are under-cooked.

Source: Community Education Trust.

Chicken (or beef)

Ingredients

2-3 lb (900-1350 grms) chicken cut into portions
1 clove garlic, crushed   )
Half teaspoon thyme   )
Salt to taste   ) for
Black pepper   ) marinade
1 tablespoon soy sauce   )
1 medium onion, chopped)
1 green pepper, sliced   )
4 oz (112 grms) oil for frying chicken
Water
Half can tomatoes OR
2 tablespoons tomato ketchup

3-4 servings

Method

1. The night before cooking, marinade chicken pieces in the marinading mixture making sure that the chicken is well covered.
2. Leave marinading chicken in the refrigerator overnight in an airtight container.

On the day of cooking:

1. Remove the chicken pieces from the seasoning and fry until brown in the oil.
2. Drain off most of the oil and then add the seasoning that the chicken was marinaded in, plus just enough water to cover it.
3. Bring to the boil and then reduce the heat.
4. Add the tomatoes or ketchup to thicken the gravy.
5. Simmer gently until the chicken is cooked (approximately 25 minutes).

Source: Community Education Trust.

Escoveitched fish

Ingredients

2 lbs (900 grms) cleaned fresh fish
1 lime or ½ lemon
2 teaspoons salt
1 teaspoon ground black pepper
4 oz (125 millilitres) oil
¼ lb (125 grms) onion
¼ lb (125 grms) carrots
2 stalks spring onions
2 cloves garlic
1 ripe red pimiento or cayenne
6 grains whole allspice

2 tablespoons water   )
2 tablespoons vinegar) Mix
½ teaspoon salt   )
2 teaspoons sugar   )

Method

1. Clean, rinse and pat dry fish.
2. Wipe prepared fish with lime or lemon juice.
3. Sprinkle with salt and ground pepper inside and outside for whole fish and on all sides for steaks and fillets.
4. Let sit for 20-30 minutes.
5. Fry in shallow hot oil until lightly brown and flesh flakes easily.
6. Set aside on a platter.
7. (Meanwhile prepare julienne of carrots, chopped spring onions, onion-rings, slivers of red pepper and mashed garlic.)
8. Drain away oil remaining in frying pan and pour in vinegar mixture.
9. Lower flame and heat gently.
10. Add vegetables and whole allspice.
11. Simmer for five minutes or until vegetables are tender but crisp.
12. Arrange fish in deep dish alternating with layers of vegetables/vinegar mixture.
13. Garnish with onion rings.
14. Let sit at room temperature 8-24 hours.
15. Serve with bread or roast potatoes.

Serves 6.

Source: Scientific Research Council, Jamaica

Pineapple fool

Ingredients

12 oz or 336 grms finely chopped fresh pineapple
  (or mango)
3/8 pint or 2 decilitres double cream
1-3 tablespoons icing sugar
½ teaspoon vanilla essence

4 servings

Method

1. Place the chopped pineapple in a sieve or colander set over a bowl and let it drain for at least 10 minutes.
2. Whip the cream in a large chilled bowl with a whisk or a rotary egg beater until it is stiff enough to hold its shape softly.
3. Taste the pineapple and sprinkle it with 1-3 tablespoons icing sugar, depending upon the pineapple's sweetness and your own taste.
4. Add the vanilla and continue beating until the cream is stiff enough to form firm, unwavering peaks on the whisk when it is lifted from the bowl.
5. Chill the whipped cream and pineapple separately until you need to serve them.
6. Fold the pineapple into the cream with a rubber spatula at the last possible moment, blending them together thoroughly but gently.
7. Spoon the fool into chilled individual bowls or sundae glasses and serve immediately.

Source: "The cooking of the Caribbean Islands" by Linda Wolfe and the editors of Time-Life Books

CENTRAL AMERICA

Guatemala

Population	7.3 million
Area	109,000 sq. km. 42,000 sq. miles
Arable land	1,834,000 hectares 4,531,000 acres
Life expectation	1960, 47 years; 1980, 59 years
Infant mortality	1960, 92 deaths 1980, 70 deaths
Population increase rate	3%
Labour force in agriculture	54%
Urbanisation	1960, 33%; 1980, 39%
Big city	Guatemala City, the capital 1.1 million
Food index	112%
Daily calorie supply per head	2156 calories, 92%
Basic food crops	Maize
Major exports	Bananas
Income per head	£459
Adult literacy	Not available
Climate	Subtropical

Honduras

Population	3.7 million
Area	112,000 sq. km. 43,200 sq. miles
Arable land	1,757,000 hectares 4,341,000 acres
Life expectation	1960, 46 years; 1980, 58 years
Infant mortality	1960, 145 deaths 1980, 88 deaths
Population increase rate	3.4%
Labour force in agriculture	62%
Urbanisation	1960, 23%; 1980, 36%
Big city	Tegulcigalpa, the capital, 300,000
Food index	82%
Daily calorie supply per head	2015 calories, 93%
Basic food crop	Maize
Major exports	Bananas, coffee
Income per head	£238
Adult literacy	About 60%
Climate	Tropical on coast, moderate inland

20

Fresh corn soup

Ingredients

Fresh corn cut from 2-3 cobs
1 cup boiling water
2 oz (56 grms) margarine or butter
2 oz (56 grms) flour
Half teaspoon salt
Pinch pepper
Small onion, finely chopped
1 pint (0.56 litre) milk

4 servings

Method

1. Cook the corn in the water until the corn is tender (about 10 minutes)
2. Melt the fat and blend in the flour.
3. Add the milk gradually, stirring constantly.
4. Add salt, pepper, onion, corn and remaining water.
5. Bring to the boil to thicken, stirring all the time, and cook gently for several minutes.
6. Taste and add more seasoning if necessary.

Source: Angela Greenwood, recipe reproduced with permission from "CIIR Overseas Volunteer News".

In Guatemala the soup would be eaten with tortillas (flat maize pancakes). A poor family would eat only soup with tortillas.

Maize tortillas

Ingredients

8 oz (224 grms) maize flour
Salt
Water

Method

1. Mix the ingredients to a soft dough and pat into round shapes about 1/4" to 1/8" (0.3 cm) thick and 5" (15 cm) across.
2. Cook on a griddle with a little margarine.
3. Wrap in a clean cloth when cooked to keep warm and retain moisture.
4. Use immediately.

Source: Pat Diskett

Baked bananas

Ingredients

4 medium semi-ripe bananas
Butter
Brown sugar or honey
Lemon or lime juice
Sour cream (optional)
4 servings

Method

1. Peel and place the bananas in a buttered baking dish.
2. Put dabs of butter on the bananas.
3. Sprinkle them liberally with brown sugar and lemon or lime juice.
4. Bake for 40 minutes at 250°F., Gas Mark 4, turning the bananas once when they are half done.
5. Serve with sour cream and honey if you like.

Source: Angela Greenwood

Bean casserole (Frijoles)

Ingredients

8 oz-12 oz (224-336 grms) dried red kidney beans (or a tin of red kidney beans)
1 red Oxo cube
1 large onion
1 tin tomatoes
1 clove garlic
4-5 oz (112-140 grms) bacon off-cuts
1 green pepper
Chilli seasoning to taste
4 oz (112 grms) mushrooms (optional)
Mixed herbs (optional)

Method

1. Soak the beans overnight.
2. Throw away the water. Wash the beans and cook them in Oxo stock with mixed herbs.
3. Boil the beans for about 90 minutes or till they are really soft.
4. Then drain and cover. Use the beans the same day or store in the fridge overnight.
5. Peel and slice the onions, chop the green pepper and crush the garlic.
6. Fry the bacon till it is crisp and add the onion, green peppers and garlic.
7. When the onion is slightly brown, add the beans and tinned tomatoes, and mushrooms if used. Stir using a wooden spoon and press the beans a little. Opening them improves the flavour.
8. Add the chilli seasoning and cook over a low heat for about 20 minutes till everything is cooked, adding extra stock if the mixture appears too dry.
9. Serve the beans hot with fresh bread or tortillas.

Source: Pat Diskett

Nicaragua

Population	2.6 million
Area	130,000 sq. km. 50,000 sq. miles
Arable land	1,516,000 hectares
	3,746,000 acres
Life expectation	1960, 47 years; 1980, 56 years
Infant mortality	1960, 144 deaths
	1980, 91 deaths
Population increase rate	3.4%
Labour force in agriculture	42%
Urbanisation	1960, 41%; 1980, 53%
Big city	Managua, the capital, 500,000
Food index	95%
Daily calorie supply per head	2446 calories, 116%
Basic food crops	Maize
Major exports	Coffee
Income per head	£314
Adult literacy	90% (approximately)
Climate	Tropical

Up till July 1979, 600 of Nicaragua's people controlled more than half of the land. The corrupt dictator Somoza himself controlled more than one third of the country's cultivated land. When Somoza was overthrown by the Sandinista Front for National Liberation in 1979, he left behind him a $1.6 billion national debt, a bankrupt economy, and a countryside devastated by war.

The country, which had traditionally been able to feed itself, suffered from a severe food shortage as a result of the war of liberation.

Since the revolution, Somoza's land has been redistributed to landless people, and a programme for agricultural development introduced making available credit facilities, machinery, seeds, fertilizers and technical education. Much of the land in Nicaragua is privately owned, but all commodities for export are sold to nationalised trading agencies.

A major achievement has been the world's biggest literacy campaign completed in 1980. Illiteracy was reduced from 80% to 20% in two years. The campaign was followed by the most ambitious adult basic education programme of any Third World country. Teaching methods and materials are designed to use students' own lives as the basis of learning, and to encourage students to take action.

An Oxfam-assisted project

Beans are the second most important food in Nicaragua after maize, and the main source of protein. But as recently as 1980 half the beans eaten had to be imported. Under the Somoza regime priority was given to export crops like cotton, sugar and coffee, and local food requirements were neglected. Now the new government has taken over unused land, and new peasant co-operatives and State farms have boosted food production dramatically. Rice and beans doubled output in 1981/82 compared with three years previously, and maize production increased by 50%.

Oxfam has helped with this programme in a small way on some 230 acres of land within the city boundary. Previously owned by the Somoza family but left idle for possible building projects, a number of plots were cleared and rotovated by machinery ready for food growing. Red beans have been grown, producing employment for around 150 men. Oxfam funds provided all preparation and cultivation costs, which worked out at about £100 an acre. Yields proved satisfactory, and a profit of some 20% was achieved. Half the profits were retained by the Ministry for further planting, and half is being used for social purposes — for the construction of toilets and for the purchase of first aid kits.

Tortilla rollups

Ingredients

1 medium onion, chopped
1 large tomato, chopped
1 oz (28 grms) butter
2 lb (900 grms) cooked pork, cut in small pieces
12-18 tortillas , warmed
½ level teaspoon salt
¼ level teaspoon Cayenne pepper
6 oz (168 grm) tin tortilla sauce or tomato sauce
1 egg,well beaten
1 banana, sliced
Grated rind of 1 orange

12 to 18 servings

Method

1. Cook onion and tomato in butter in a large frying pan until the onion is done.
2. Add meat, 1 tortilla cut in thin strips, salt, pepper and sauce.
3. Simmer for 10-15 minutes, stirring frequently.
4. Add egg, banana and orange rind.
5. Continue simmering for 10 minutes, stirring constantly.
6. Place 1-2 tablespoons of the mixture on each tortilla and roll.
7. Arrange on a heated serving dish, placing join on underside.
8. Pour remainder of meat mixture over tortilla rolls and serve as appetisers.

Source: 'The Cookbook of the United Nations' by Barbara Kraus

Pork and fruit

Ingredients

¾ pint (0.32 litre) boiling water
2 lb (about 900 grms) pork fillets, cut up
1 oz (28 grms) butter
1 large onion, chopped
3 tomatoes, chopped
1 chilli
¼ level teaspoon Cayenne pepper
6 bay leaves
3 level tablespoons rice
About half a pint (0.28 litre) water
3 slices pineapple, cut in chunks
2 ripe bananas, sliced
Brown sugar and salt

6 servings

Method

1. Fry pork in butter in a 10-12 inch (25-30 cm) frying pan.
2. As pork browns, remove from butter to saucepan.
3. Add onions, tomatoes and chillies to pan in which pork was browned and simmer for about 5 minutes.
4. Add Cayenne pepper, bay leaves and rice, and cook until thick.
5. Add water, pineapple, bananas and meat to the sauce.
6. Cover and simmer gently for 30 minutes or until meat is tender.
7. Stir frequently and add water if necessary.
8. Add salt and sugar to taste if necessary.

Source: adapted from 'The Cookbook of the United Nations' by Barbara Kraus

Chile

Salvador Allende, the world's first democratically elected Marxist head of state, was overthrown by a brutal military coup in 1973. While he was in power, a profound land reform took place, mainly aimed at breaking up large holdings and distributing land to the peasants. Certain industries were nationalised, including the two most important copper mines. Chile is estimated to have one quarter of the world's copper reserves.

The military government aims to get maximum economic growth and heavy foreign and domestic private investment. Much of the land affected by the reform has since been sold to private interests.

The government wants to sell fruit and vegetables abroad, but there have been sharp declines in agricultural production in recent years. Wheat production has halved since 1970/1 and massive amounts have had to be imported. Meanwhile over one million peasants, about 40% of the rural population, still work tiny scattered and inefficient smallholdings and rural unemployment is rising rapidly.

An Oxfam-supported project

Earning a living is often hard in Chile's cities too, and many people are either unemployed or underemployed.

In the Puento Alto district of the town of Chiguayante, a church group from amongst the poorest communities has bought a disused bakehouse which they are in the process of restoring. Bread is an important staple in the Chilean diet and yet in this part of the town there are no bakeries. Supplies brought in from the big commercial bakeries are expensive and often of poor quality. Several members of the group are unemployed bakers and initially three of them — all master bakers — will bring the bakehouse back into production. Once established, they hope to form a co-operative incorporating other unemployed bakers. Their market is assured — in an area where most families are struggling against desperate poverty, a source of cheap, nutritious bread gives a vital boost to their diet. As well as providing for local families, the bakery will supply the church's kindergarten which takes in over 240 children.

The bakery project is just one of the initiatives helping poor communities in Puento Alto. A joint committee of OXFAM, CAFOD and Christian Aid supported it with a loan of £2,565 for working capital and to buy equipment. This will be repaid into a community fund to be used for other projects — health, education and job-creation schemes.

Population	11.1 million
Area	757,000 sq. km. 292,000 sq. miles
Arable land	5,530,000 hectares 13,664,000 acres
Life expectation	1960, 57 years; 1980, 67 years
Infant mortality	1960, 114 deaths; 1980, 43 deaths
Population increase rate	1.7%
Labour force in agriculture	18%
Urbanisation	1960, 68%; 1980, 80%
Big city	Santiago, the capital, 2.6 mn.
Food index	93%
Daily calorie supply per head	2656 calories, 110%
Basic food crops	Wheat
Major exports	Copper
Income per head	£914
Adult literacy	Not known
Climate	Temperate

Maize pie

Ingredients

2 onions
2 tablespoons butter
2 cups minced meat
½ cup meat stock
½ cup seedless raisins
1 teaspoon cumin seed
1 teaspoon oregano or marjoram
Salt and pepper to taste
20 ripe olives
2 hardboiled eggs
3 cobs maize, grated, or 1 can creamed sweet corn
2 beaten eggs
2 tablespoons sugar
Dash of flour
1 teaspoon salt
¼ teaspoon pepper
1½ cups milk

3–4 servings

Method

1. Chop onions and sauté in butter.
2. Add meat and stock.
3. Stir in the raisins, spices, salt and pepper.
4. Simmer for 30 minutes.
5. Place mixture in a pyrex dish or casserole.
6. Scatter olives and sliced hardboiled eggs over it.
7. In another bowl place the grated maize or creamed canned corn.
8. Add the beaten eggs, sugar, flour, salt, pepper and milk.
9. Stir together and pour over the meat.
10. Bake 45 minutes in the oven at 350°F (Gas Mark 3) or until well browned.

Source: 'Cookbook'. Recipes collected by the American Women's Literary Club of Lima, Peru.

Empañadas (Meat pies)

Ingredients

1 lb (450 grms) plain flour
3 eggs, lightly beaten
½ lb (225 grms) suet, finely chopped
Water to mix
1 level tablespoon salt
2 large onions, chopped
2 lbs (900 grms) beef or boned chicken, raw or cooked, chopped
2 oz (56 grms) sweet red pepper, chopped
32 small stuffed olives
3 oz (84 grms) raisins
2 hardboiled eggs, coarsely chopped

16 empañadas

Method

1. Combine the flour, eggs and half the suet.
2. Mix in salted water till dough can be rolled into very thin sheets.
3. Put the onion, beef or chicken, red pepper and remaining suet in a frying pan.
4. Stir and fry till the onions and meat are tender.
5. Roll out the dough into very thin sheets, and cut into 5 inch (13 cm) squares for individual empañadas.
6. Place a heaped tablespoon of onion and meat mixture, olives, a few raisins, and chopped egg on each square.
7. Fold dough over meat and press edges together.
8. Place on a baking sheet and bake for about 30 minutes in a very moderate oven (325°F. Mark 2-3).

Source: 'The Cookbook of the United Nations', by Barbara Kraus

Population	976,700,000
Area	9,561,000 sq. km.
	3,691,500 sq. miles
Arable land	99,200,000 hectares
	245,123,200 acres
Life expectation	1960, not known;
	1980, 64 years
Infant mortality	1960, not known
	1980, 56 deaths
Population increase rate	1.8%
Labour force in agriculture	58%
Urbanisation	1960, not known; 1980, 13%
Biggest cities	Beijing, the capital, 8.5 mn.
	Shanghai, 12.5 mn.
Food index	116%
Daily calorie supply per head	2441 calories, 103%
Basic food crops	Rice, wheat, maize
Major exports	Manufacturing (especially textile yarn and fabrics) and agricultural products (especially grain and livestock)
Income per head	£123
Adult literacy	About 66%
Climate	Continental, with extremes of temperature. Subtropical in the South East

Before the revolution of 1949, China was known as the land of famine. Most of the population — perhaps 80% — lived lives of great poverty and hardship, trying to scratch a living from tiny plots of land for which they often had to pay very high rents.

Post-revolutionary China has put emphasis on ordinary people getting control of land, seed, water, fertiliser and credit and on meeting people's basic needs.

China provides one of the best examples of a land reform which has really benefited the vast majority of the population. Inequality has been reduced and economic advance achieved. The standard of living of the vast majority of the population has been greatly improved.

China has apparently also had impressive achievements in overcoming the appalling ecological consequences of thousands of years of forest destruction. Forest restoration has been a major preoccupation of the Chinese government since 1949.

Oxfam's work in China

China has sought to be self-reliant. But Oxfam has been able to make three small grants since 1979: £5,000 for supplies for flood victims in Sichuan province; £15,000 for a fishery co-operative for refugees from Vietnam, and £15,000 for a refugee school.

Sliced beef with green peppers

Ingredients

200 grms or about 8 oz lean beef
2 cloves garlic
½ teaspoon salt
1 teaspoon sugar
¼ teaspoon baking powder
2 teaspoons sesame oil
1 tablespoon oyster sauce
1 tablespoon cornflour
Ground pepper
2 large green peppers
200 millilitres or 7 ½ fluid oz vegetable oil
1 tablespoon dark soya sauce
1 tablespoon peanut oil
½ tablespoon fermented black beans (sold in a tin)
1 tablespoon Chinese wine or dry white cooking
   wine
1 tablespoon light soya sauce

Method

1. Cut meat into small thin slices and season with salt, pepper, sugar, baking powder, dark sauce and oil for one hour.
2. Remove seeds from green pepper and chop into fairly large pieces.
3. Crush garlic.
4. Deep fry beef for approximately 20 seconds, then remove and drain.
5. Pour off most of the oil from the pan and then put in beef with the green pepper, garlic, black beans.
6. Stir fry over medium heat for 12 minutes.
7. Add oyster sauce and light sauce, and wine.
8. Stir for one more minute.
9. Then add cornflour paste and serve immediately onto a platter.
10. Sprinkle heated sesame oil over the dish.

Source: ''The flavour of Hong Kong''.

Minced spiced beef with bean curd.

Ingredients

200 grms or about 8 oz. minced beef
100 grms or about 4 oz bean curd
3 small red onions
3 small chillies
1'' (3 cm) knob root ginger
2 cloves garlic
100 millilitres or about 3 ½ fluid oz vegetable oil
50 millilitres or about 2 fluid oz beef stock
2 spring onions
1 tablespoon Chinese wine (dry white wine will do)
2 tablespoons dark soya sauce
½ teaspoon salt
¼ teaspoon pepper
2 teaspoons seame oil
1 tablespoon black beans
1 tablespoon oyster sauce
1 tablespoon light soy sauce
1 tablespoon chilli sauce
1 tablespoon cornflour

Method

1. Mix beef with wine, dark sauce, salt and pepper.
2. Leave for 20 minutes.
3. Cut bean curd into 1'' (3 cm) squares.
4. Chop red onions, chillies and ginger.
5. Crush garlic and black beans.
6. Deep fry bean curd for 2-3 minutes in vegetable oil and stir frequently.
7. Then remove and drain the ingredients.
8. Pour most of oil from frying pan and add beef, onions, chillies, ginger, garlic, and black beans.
9. Stir fry for 2 minutes.
10. Add cornflour made into a paste with water and bean curd, and stir well for one minute.
11. Sprinkle sesame oil over the food: then arrange it in a serving dish.
12. Cut the spring onions in 1'' (3 cm) lengths and place on top.

Source: ''The flavour of Hong Kong''.

Spiced spare ribs

Ingredients

2 lb or about 450 grms spare ribs, separated and
  cut in serving pieces
Pineapple sliced)
Red chillis   ) for garnishing
Chinese celery

for marinade

2 teaspoons sweet bean sauce
¼ teaspoon black pepper
½ teaspoon Five Spice Powder
4 cloves garlic
2 fluid oz (60 millilitres) water
1½ tablespoons light soy sauce

Method

1. Marinade spare ribs for 30 minutes.
2. Place the spare ribs in a roasting pan and roast
   in a preheated oven on Gas Mark 6 (400°F or
   204°C.).
3. Turn after 30 minutes and add some water if
   the meat is too dry and baste over, till the
   spare ribs are well done.
4. Remove the ribs, garnish and serve.

Source: 'The Hong Kong Cookbook' published by Vista
    Productions, Hong Kong.

Chicken in tin foil

Ingredients

2 spring or young chickens (each cut into 6 pieces)
6 slices ham
6 slices fresh root ginger, peeled
6 heads of spring onions (each 2½ " or about 7 cm
  long)
6 pieces tin foil (each 3" or about 8 cm square)

for marinade

Pinch of 5 spice powder   )
4 tablespoons of cooking wine (dry) mixed
  white wine will do)   ) together
4 tablespoons light soy sauce   )
¼ teaspoon peppercorns, ground   )

Method

1. Marinade chicken pieces, ginger slices and
   spring onions for 15 minutes.
2. Place 1 slice ham, 2 chicken pieces and 1 each
   of the ginger slices and onions on a piece of
   tin foil.
3. Fold the foil to enclose.
4. Do the same thing with the rest of the
   ingredients.
5. Put the filled tin foil on a baking tray and place
   in a preheated oven at Gas Mark 2.
6. Bake for 15-20 minutes, remove and serve.

Source: 'The Hong Kong Cookbook', published by Vista
    Productions, Hong Kong.

Shrimps or prawns in hot garlic sauce

Ingredients

400 grms (about 13 oz) shrimps (or prawns)
1 egg white
2 cloves garlic, chopped
25 millilitres (a large tablespoon) Chinese wine (or dry cooking wine)
1 brown onion
3 red chillies
400 millilitres (about 13 fluid oz) vegetable oil
2 small spring onions
1'' knob fresh root ginger, peeled and chopped
125 millilitres (4 fluid oz) fish stock
½ teaspoon salt
1 teaspoon sesame oil
1 tablespoon cornflour
1 teaspoon salt
1 tablespoon black bean paste
1 tablespoon light soy sauce

Method

1. Gut the shrimps, and cut them in half lengthwise.
2. Lightly beat the egg white and add the wine, half the cornflour and salt, and mix well.
3. Add the shrimps and marinade for 30 minutes.
4. Finely chop brown onions, spring onions, chillies, ginger and garlic.
5. Heat vegetable oil and spoon in the coated shrimps.
6. Deep fry for about 2 minutes until the shrimps turn pink.
7. Remove shrimps, drain and set aside in a warm place.
8. Pour off most of the oil, then add onions, chillies, ginger and garlic and place over moderate heat for 5 minutes, stirring constantly.
9. Add stock, bean paste, soy sauce and sugar and bring to the boil.
10. Replace the shrimps, lower heat, simmer gently for 2-3 minutes.
11. Mix cornflour paste and add to the pan and thicken.
12. Arrange on serving dish, and sprinkle with sesame oil.

Source: 'The flavour of Hong Kong'.

Minced pork balls with cabbage

Ingredients

400 grms or about 1 lb pork
200 grms or about 8 oz chopped cabbage
200 millilitres or about 6½ fluid oz chicken stock
1 teaspoon light soya sauce
Ground pepper
½ teaspoon salt
¼ teaspoon pepper
2 eggs
1 tablespoon cornflour

Method

1. Mince the pork, season with salt, pepper, and soya sauce.
2. Beat eggs and mix with pork.
3. Divide meat into small balls.
4. Fry the balls over a medium heat until they are golden brown and cooked.
5. Then remove the balls and keep them warm.
6. Add cabbage to the pan and stir fry for 1-2 minutes.
7. Pour in stock, bring to the boil, and replace the balls.
8. Season with pepper, simmer until stock is reduced by one half.
9. Add cornflour paste to thicken.

Source: 'The flavour of Hong Kong.'

Eggplant in hot garlic sauce

Ingredients

1 eggplant (about 500 grms or 1 lb)
2 spring onions
2 chillies
100 millilitres (about 3 fluid oz) peanut oil
100 millilitres stock
1 teaspoon sugar
½ teaspoon salt
1 teaspoon vinegar
1'' knob (2½ cm) peeled fresh ginger
3 garlic cloves, peeled
60 grms (about 3 oz) minced beef
1 tablespoon light soy sauce
¼ teaspoon pepper
2 teaspoons cornflour
1 teaspoon sesame oil

Method

1. Cut eggplant on the bias into thin slices (so you get longer strips).
2. Chop spring onions, ginger and chillies; crush the garlic.
3. Gently fry the eggplant in peanut oil for 3-4 minutes until it is soft.
4. Then remove the eggplant and drain it.
5. Pour away most of the oil from the pan and then add onions, ginger, chillies, garlic and mince.
6. Stir well for one minute.
7. Then add soya sauce, sugar, salt, pepper and stock.
8. Bring to the boil, add eggplant; lower heat and simmer until the liquid is reduced by one half.
9. Add cornflour paste to thicken.
10 Just before serving, stir in vinegar and sesame oil.

Source: 'The flavour of Hong Kong'.

Stirfried quick braised double winter

Ingredients

10 medium dried Chinese winter mushrooms soaked in warm water for 30 minutes and stalks removed)
5 oz or 155 grms winter bamboo shoots
2 tablespoons vegetable oil
2 tablespoons light soya sauce
1½ teaspoons sugar
6 tablespoons chicken broth
2 teaspoons cornflour (blended in 2 tablespoons water)
1 teaspoon sesame oil

Method

1. Quarter the mushrooms and cut the bamboo shoots into wedge shaped pieces half an inch (about 1 cm) thick.
2. Heat vegetable oil in a frying pan and when it is very hot, lower the heat and add the bamboo shoots.
3. Stirfry for half a minute, add soya sauce and sugar.
4. After stirring and tossing for 2-3 minutes add the mushrooms and chicken broth.
5. Stir gently and cook together for 3 minutes.
6. Add cornflour mixture.
7. When the sauce has thickened, sprinkle with sesame oil and serve.

Note: This dish is associated with Spring in Shanghai. It is common in China to serve winter products in the warmer seasons.

Source: P.182 'Chinese Food, by Kenneth Lo' copyright (c) Kenneth Lo, published by Penguin Books Ltd., and reprinted by their permission.

Toffee apples and bananas

Ingredients

2 large cooking apples
100 grms (about 3½ oz) plain flour
150 grms (about 5 oz) sugar
25 grms (about 1 oz) sesame seeds
3 bananas
500 millilitres (16 fluid oz) vegetable oil
100 millilitres (about 3 fluid oz) peanut oil
Iced water

Method

1. Peel and core apples and cut into wedges.
2. Skin the bananas, cut into quarters, first lengthwise, then across.
3. Mix flour with enough water to form a smooth batter, and with it coat the apples and banana pieces.
4. Deep fry the fruits for 2-3 minutes until they are golden brown.
5. In a saucepan heat the peanut oil, add sugar and 100 millilitres water.
6. Stir the oil, sugar and water until the sugar dissolves.
7. Add the fried fruits and mix until they are evenly coated with syrup.
8. Remove, sprinkle with sesame seeds and plunge immediately into iced water to set the syrup hard

Source: 'The flavour of Hong Kong'

Szechuan date pancakes

Ingredients

150 grms (about 5 oz) dates
100 grms (about 3½ oz) sweet bean paste
150 grms (about 5 oz) sugar
25 millilitres (large tablespoon) peanut oil

Pancake

150 grms (about 5 oz) plain flour
2 eggs
25 grms (just under 1 oz) butter
25 millilitres milk
500 millilitres (about 16 fluid oz) vegetable oil
½ teaspoon sugar

Method

1. Chop dates into small pieces, place in a saucepan together with sugar.
2. Add just enough water to cover and bring to the boil.
3. Simmer gently for 4-5 minutes until the sugar dissolves.
4. Pass through a fine sieve, mix with bean paste.
5. Heat oil in wok, add mixture and stir for 2-3 minutes over low heat.
6. Remove from heat and drain away the oil.
7. Make a thin batter by mixing together flour, milk, eggs and butter.
8. If the batter is too thick add a little extra milk or cold water.
9. Add a little batter to a large greased frying pan or skillet and cook until just set.
10. Remove the pancake and repeat the process.
11. Spread equal portions of mixture in the pan, fold and seal.
12. Deep fry until golden brown. Cut into three pieces and serve.

Source: 'The flavour of Hong Kong'

Colombia

The population is made up of a small minority of aboriginal Amerindian tribal people plus the descendants of the Spanish and of black slaves imported to work the sugar plantations , and people of mixed race. There is a wide gap between the very rich and the poor peasants and shanty town dwellers. Many rural families eke out a living on the breadline in the mountains and coastal plain. The high urbanisation figures are due partly to widespread evacuation of the countryside by tenants and sharecroppers as land is concentrated in fewer and fewer hands.

An Oxfam-supported project

The isolated communities among the mangrove swamps of the Pacific coast of Colombia are some of the most forgotten people of South America. Of African origin, slaves who were brought over by the Spaniards to work the plantations, these black groups eke out an existence by fishing and subsistence agriculture.

They live a precarious existence under the constant threat of flooding from a high rainfall and high tides. Yet obtaining fresh uncontaminated water for drinking and cooking is a major problem. As a consequence the incidence of disease is high.

Oxfam has helped a number of communities with schemes to obtain 'sweet' water. In some areas it has been possible to sink wells relying on the natural filtration of the sandy soil. In some communities tanks to collect and store rainwater were the only practical possibility. And in a few where groups were living near a spring or clean stream, a piped water supply was possible. One such was Concepcion, a community of 800 people who worked with a professional builder in 1981 to pipe water from a spring above their village. £752 from Oxfam paid for the piping, cement, transport and builder's salary.

Population	26.7 million
Area	1,139,000 sq. km
	439,000 sq. miles
Arable land	5,650,000 hectares
	13,961,000 acres
Life expectation	1960, 53 years; 1980, 63 years
Infant mortality	1960, 93 deaths;
	1980, 56 deaths
Population increase rate	2.3%
Labour force in agriculture	26%
Urbanisation	1960, 48%; 1980, 70%
Big city	Bogota, the capital, 4.3 mn.
Food index	122%
Daily calorie supply per head	2364 calories, 98%
Basic food crops	Rice, maize
Major exports	Coffee, marijuana, cocaine
Income per head	£502
Adult literacy	Not known
Climate	Tropical on coastland, temperate on plateau

Sopa de ajiaco de papas

(Potato soup)

Ingredients

6 chicken breasts
2½ pints (about 1.4 litres) water
1 onion, finely chopped
4-5 sprigs parsley, very finely chopped
Few sprigs of rosemary (optional)
Salt and pepper
1 large floury potato, diced
4 medium-sized boiling potatoes, diced
Parsley sprigs

Serves 6-8 people

Method

1. Cover chicken with cold water.
2. Add onion, chopped parsley, rosemary, salt and pepper.
3. Simmer until chicken is tender.
4. After half an hour, add floury potato so that it will disintegrate and give body to the soup.
5. Add the rest of the potatoes about 15 minutes before serving the soup, so that pieces will be tender but not too soft.
6. Garnish with sprigs of parsley.

Source: 'Cookbook of the United Nations', by Barbara Kraus

Cyprus

Population	623,000 people
Area	9,251 sq. km. 3,572 sq. miles
Arable land	432,000 hectares; 1,067,000 acres
Life expectation	1960, 69 years; 1980, 73 years
Infant mortality	1960, not known; 1980, 18
Population increase rate	0.6% (1970-79)
Labour force in agriculture	33%
Urbanisation	1980, 46%
Capital	Nicosia (147,000 people)
Food index	100%
Daily calorie intake as percentage of requirements in 1977	139%
Basic food crops	Wheat, barley
Major exports	Potatoes, table wines, citrus fruits, clothing, cement, footwear
Income per head	£1514
Adult literacy	89%
Climate	Mediterranean

Economically the island has suffered remarkably little throughout the troubles of the last decade. Most of the economy has always been in Greek Cypriot hands.

Oxfam's most recent grant was in 1977/8 to help refugees.

Youvarlacia soup

(Soup with meatballs)

Ingredients

for the meatballs

500 grms. or about 1 lb 2 oz minced meat
1 clove garlic, finely chopped
1 tablespoon onion, finely chopped
1 egg
¼ cup rice
½ cup flour
1 teaspoon parsley, finely chopped

for the liquid

¼ cup rice
8 cups chicken broth
2 egg yolks
Juice of 2 lemons
Salt to taste

6-8 servings

Method

1. Put the minced meat into a bowl and add garlic, onion, egg, parsley and half the rice.
2. Knead well.
3. Form into small balls and sprinkle with flour.
4. Put the broth in a pan and heat well.
5. Add the meat balls and remaining rice.
6. Simmer for about 30 minutes until they are cooked.
7. Beat the egg yolks together with the lemon juice and then gradually add 2 cups broth from the pan, beating the mixture continuously.
8. Return the broth to the pan and add salt to taste.
9. Boil for about 5 minutes.
10. Serve 4-5 meatballs to each dish of soup.

Source: Cyprus High Commission

Village salad

Ingredients

Some leaves of lettuce
1 onion cut in slices
2-3 small cucumbers or 1 large
2-3 medium tomatoes
50 grms of feta cheese
some black olives
Pickled caper leaves
Oil, lemon, salt, dried mint

Method

1. Clean and cut the ingredients and place in a large bowl.
2. Add oil, lemon and seasoning.
3. Finally sprinkle some small pieces of feta cheese on top.

Source: Cyprus High Commission

Aubergine moussaka

Ingredients

1 lb. 6 oz. (616 grms) aubergines
12 oz. (336 grms) minced meat, lamb or beef
Half a minced onion
Parsley
A little tomato purée
Breadcrumbs
Olive oil for frying

sauce

3 tablespoons butter or margarine
3½—4 tablespoons flour
2 cups milk
1 egg
Salt and pepper
1 tablespoon grated cheese

3 servings

Method

1. Slice the aubergines, sprinkle them with salt and leave them to dry.
2. Fry them in butter or olive oil if possible.
3. Fry 12 oz (336 grms) minced meat in butter or oil, with half minced onion, parsley and a little tomato puree.
4. Grease a baking dish and coat it with breadcrumbs.
5. Put in it a layer of aubergines, then the minced meat.
6. Add the remaining aubergines and cover with the thick sauce (recipe below).
7. To the sauce add a few breadcrumbs and a little melted butter.
8. Brown in the oven.

Sauce

1. Melt the butter. Add the flour little by little and stir until dissolved.
2. Remove the pan from the stove, add the milk and cook till all the flour dissolves and it is cooked thoroughly.
3. Stir the sauce continuously until it becomes like custard; add cheese and egg. (This recipe is half the quantity originally recommended.)

Egypt

The building of the Aswan dam, controlling the river Nile's average level and its floods has made it possible to cultivate 1.2 million acres and to use large areas for irrigated crops. A fishing industry has been created on the lake.

But there have been serious disadvantages. The absence of silt in the Nile valley has led to the deepening of the river bed, inroads on the coast along the delta and the disappearance of sardines on the Alexandria coast. Enormous quantities of expensive artificial fertiliser have had to be used to replace the fertilising elements contained in the silt which is now threatening to fill up Lake Nasser more quickly than was anticipated. Some of the irrigated land has become saline and the disease called bilharzia has reached parts of Egypt where it had previously been unknown.

An Oxfam-supported project

When the Aswan High Dam was built and Lake Nasser flooded the fertile river valley above the dam, groups of Bushari and Ababda nomads lost part of their traditional summer pastures. As a result thousands of their animals died, and the nomads have suffered considerable hardship ever since.

In the late seventies a small group of nomads moved to the Allaqui area, and now a settlement programme is underway. Mud houses are being built by the people under the guidance of local masons. A school and evening classes have been started, and a first-aid nurse has been appointed. Wells are being dug, and gardens started.

The nomads are keeping some of their animals, but the plan is that from growing fruit and vegetables they will be able to obtain an additional source of income as well as to eat better themselves.

The first gardeners have grown okra, beans, and peas which they can eat fresh or dry, and cucumbers and tomatoes. Fruit and other trees are being raised in the project nursery, and already several settlers have established lemon, orange and guava trees. Both Oxfam and Christian Aid are contributing to this programme.

Population	39.8 million
Area	1,001,000 sq. km or 386,400 sq. miles
Arable land	2,855,000 hectares 7,051,000 acres
Life expectation	1960, 46 years; 1980, 57 years
Infant mortality	1960, 128 deaths; 1980, 103 deaths
Population increase rate	2.1%
Labour force in agriculture	50%
Urbanisation	1960, 38%; 1980, 45%
Big city	Cairo, the capital, 5mn.
Food index	93%
Daily calorie supply per head	2760 calories, 118%
Basic food crops	Maize, wheat, rice
Major exports	Cotton, oil
Income per head	£246
Adult literacy	44%
Climate	Hot and dry with mild winters

Meat with courgettes and chickpeas

Ingredients

2 onions, chopped
2 whole cloves garlic (optional)
2 oz. (56 grms) butter or 3 tablespoons oil
2 lb. (900 grms) lean boned stewing lamb or beef, cubed
2–3 tablespoons tomato concentrate
2 oz. (56 grms) chickpeas, soaked overnight
Salt and black pepper
1 teaspoon ground allspice (optional)
2 lb. (900 grms) courgettes, washed and sliced
(or a large English marrow, peeled and cubed)

7–8 servings

Method

1. Fry the chopped onions and whole garlic cloves in hot butter or oil until golden.
2. Add the meat cubes and brown them all over to seal in the juices.
3. Stir in the tomato concentrate.
4. Add the soaked and drained chickpeas, and cover with water.
5. Season to taste with salt, pepper and ground allspice if liked.
6. Stir well, bring to the boil and cover the pan.
7. Simmer gently for about 1½ hours.
8. Add the courgettes (or marrow) and simmer for a further half hour, or until the meat, chickpeas and vegetables are very tender and the liquid has been absorbed.
9. Add a little more water during cooking if necessary.
10. Adjust seasoning and serve.

Source: *'A book of Middle Eastern food', by Claudia Roden, published by Penguins.*

INDIAN SUB~CONTINENT

India

India gained independence from Britain in 1947. Since then laws have been introduced to limit landholdings, give land to the tiller and ensure that landowners live near their land. But landlords evade these laws and inequalities in land distribution remain great. 120 million people out of a total population of 684 million are thought to be landless.

Food production has grown faster than population since independence. But the daily food supply per head measured in calories in 1978/80 still fell below the level of 1961/5 (1998 calories; UK: 3316 calories). Yet India exported about 953,000 metric tonnes of rice in 1981.

An Oxfam-supported project in India

During and after a prolonged drought from 1899 to 1908, the adivasi (aboriginal) people of Kokanwada in western India lost most of their land to more sophisticated mainly caste Hindu people. In 1976, these landlords still owned most of the land at Kokanwada in defiance of land reform measures. Many of the Koknis (adivasi people of Kokanwada) who still held small pieces of land could not grow enough to feed themselves.

For six decades the dispossessed Koknis and their descendants had worked for the landlords as bonded or semi-bonded labourers. But with the introduction of modern farming and especially irrigated farming, the landlords preferred to use casual labourers either from inside the village or preferably from outside the area. In 1980, a local farm labourer earned three Rupees a day when the basic food, sorghum, cost Rupees 1.10 a kilogram. So the land-poor and landless Koknis were faced with a situation of chronic underemployment and unemployment.

As a result of an Oxfam-supported confidence-building project, a group of Koknis started a buffalo milk co-operative to provide employment, cash income and a little milk for domestic use. The co-op grew and flourished. In 1981 Oxfam agreed to lend the Kokanwada Milk Co-operative, which by then had about 182 members, £2,500 to extend the project to other very poor adivasis in neighbouring villages. The loan was deposited in a bank to guarantee loans for 70 landless families.

Population	673 million
Area	3,288,000 sq. km.
	1269,000 sq. miles
Arable land	169,130,000 hectares
	417,920,000 acres
Life expectation	1960, 43 years; 1980, 52 years
Infant mortality	1960, 165 deaths;
	1980, 123 deaths
Population increase rate	2.1%
Labour force in agriculture	62%
Urbanisation	1960, 18%; 1980, 22%
Major cities	Delhi, the capital, 3.3 mn.
	Madras, 3.1 mn.
	Bombay, 5.9 mn.
	Calcutta, 7 mn.
Food index	101%
Daily calorie supply per head	2021 calories, 89%
Basic food crops	Rice, wheat, millet, sorghum, maize, barley
Major exports	Jute, tea, engineering goods, iron ore
Income per head	£102
Adult literacy	36%
Climate	Wide variations: tropical climate with cooler weather in highlands

Bangladesh

Bangladesh's soil is rich but most of its people are poor. Less than 10% of rural households own over half the country's cultivable land while 60% of rural families own less than 10% of the land. About half of the families living in the countryside are landless, almost all of them farm labourers.

Food is distributed according to purchasing power. Farm labourers earn so little that they can hardly feed themselves, let alone their dependants. This is the group that has suffered most in the great famines of 1943 and 1974.

Poor women are particularly powerless in Bangladesh. They are oppressed because they are poor and also because they are female in a male-dominated Moslem society.

An Oxfam-supported project

Nijera Kori (We do it ourselves) is an Oxfam-supported project that has been working through women community workers with very poor, mainly landless women, since 1975. Some of them are beggars. Most of them drink water from an open pond.

Population	88.5 million
Area	144,000 sq. km.
	55,500 sq. miles
Arable land	9,145,000 hectares;
	22,597,000 acres
Life expectation	1960, 37 years; 1980, 46 years
Infant mortality	1960, 159 deaths;
	1980, 136 deaths
Population increase rate	2.6%
Labour force in agriculture	83%
Urbanisation	1960, 5%; 1980, 11%
Major cities	Dacca, the capital, 3.4 mn.
	Chittagong, 1.3 mn.
Food index	94%
Daily calorie supply per head	Not known
Basic food crop	Rice
Major exports	Jute
Income per head	£55
Adult literacy	26%
Climate	Tropical monsoon

The organisation aims to raise these women's self-confidence and helps them to discover and develop their abilities and skills. Each group of women chooses an activity which will enable them to earn an income. Some process paddy into rice, some buy and sell lentils, some salt and sell fish.

The project is one of the first in Bangladesh to prepare women for leadership roles as well as for development work at various levels of responsibility. Much emphasis is put on solidarity between and among women.

Sheena Grosset, then Oxfam's Field Secretary for the area, commented in 1981: ''Nijera Kori has proved to be a rather outstanding village development project. Women equipped with the necessary skills work individually or in pairs in the villages helping other women to organise themselves and develop group independence and self-confidence.''

The project's co-ordinator wrote in June 1982: ''Now the groups are more aware of their legal rights and their own strength, they have begun to speak out against injustices''.

Pakistan

One estimate indicates that only 8% of the farms use at least 42% of the farmland in Pakistan. Nearly half the population of the country is thought to be undernourished. High technology farming, encouraged by government and big international aid donors, has made worse the inequities in the countryside.

Large stretches of the hills in the Northern Provinces have been visibly deforested within the last century. On the land irrigated by water from the River Indus and its tributaries, there are tremendous problems of water-logging, salinity and siltage.

An Oxfam-supported project in Pakistan

Nirali Kitaben is a secular non-profit making publishing house. Although there is much talk in Pakistan on the setting up of mother and child care centres and the need to impart basic education to women on the subject of nutrition, child care, hygiene, family planning, child birth, etc, there is virtually no material available to help provide this education. Nirali Kitaben is the only group who have been concerned with producing simple material — small booklets designed for newly literate people, and these publications can be seen on sale in any forward-thinking voluntary hospital.

In 1982, Oxfam gave £7,572 to help Nirali Kitaben to produce flip charts, posters and a film strip as well as to buy essential audio-visual equipment. In this way, the agency hopes to help shift the present emphasis on literacy as the only means of providing education and to open up a way to reach illiterate people.

Population	82.2 million
Area	804,000 sq. km.
	310,000 sq. miles
Arable land	20,320,000 hectares
	50,210,000 acres
Life expectation	1960, 43 years; 1980, 50 years
Infant mortality	1960, 162 deaths;
	1980, 126 deaths
Population increase rate	3.1%
Labour force in agriculture	53%
Urbanisation	1960, 22%; 1980, 28%
Major cities	Islamabad, the capital, 201,000
	Karachi, 5.1 mn.
	Lahore, 2.9 mn.
Food index	101%
Daily calorie supply per head	2281 calories, 99%
Basic food crops	Wheat, rice
Major exports	Rice, cotton
Income per head	£127
Adult literacy	24%
Climate	Subtropical. Cold in high lands

Vegetarian dishes

Channa dal (Chickpeas)

Ingredients

8 oz 224 grams chickpeas
2 green chillies
1 medium onion
2 oz (56 grms) ghee, butter or margarine
Half teaspoon turmeric
1 teaspoon cummin seeds
1 teaspoon mustard seeds
2 tablespoons freshly grated coconut (or desiccated if absolutely necessary)
Salt to taste
Coriander leaves (if available) or watercress or parsley

About 3 servings

Method

1. Wash and soak the chickpeas overnight.
2. Boil till soft in a pressure cooker in salted water for about half an hour.
3. Drain them.
4. Chop the green chillies. Chop the onion finely.
5. Heat the fat and fry the onions till they are a pale golden colour.
6. Add the turmeric, cummin and mustard. When the mustard seeds begin to splutter and burst, add the chickpeas and fry.
7. Cover and cook over low heat for 10 minutes.
8. Now add the coconut and green chillies.
9. Cover and cook for 5 minutes.
10. Add the leaves at the last moment.

Source: "Cooking the Indian Way" by Attia Hosain and Sita Pasricha. Reproduced by permission of The Hamlyn Publishing Group Limited

Pea and cashew nut stew

Ingredients

8 small onions
2 cloves garlic
1 piece root ginger 1 inch (3 cm) long
¼ sweet green pepper
1 lb (448 grms) peas
8 oz (224 grms) cashew nuts
½ oz (14 grms) cooking fat or oil as necessary
pinch garam masala
1 teaspoon rice flour
1 teaspoon salt
8 tablespoons thick coconut milk made up of
    2 oz (56 grms) coconut cream (bought in a bar)
    or desiccated coconut in ¼ pt (1 decil) hot
    water

Method

1. Parboil peas in water and salt and then keep the water.
2. Meanwhile peel and chop the onions and the garlic. Peel and grate the ginger.
3. Chop the green pepper, throw away the seeds.
4. Fry the cashew nuts and remove from the pan.
5. In the same oil fry first the onions and then add gradually the garlic, ginger, spices and flour.
6. Take one third of a pint or about 150 decilitres from the hot water in which the peas have been cooked and pour over the coconut cream or desiccated coconut. Stir till the coconut is melted.
7. Pour the coconut mixture, peas, nuts and green pepper onto the mixture in the frying pan and stir. Then gently cook till the peas are quite done. You may need to add extra water from that in which the peas were cooked.

Source: "Cooking the Indian Way" by Attia Hosain and Sita Pasricha.
Reproduced by permission of The Hamlyn Publishing Group Limited

Red lentils and tomato stew

Ingredients

1 medium onion
3 cloves garlic
8 oz (225 grms) tomatoes
4 oz (112 grms) red lentils
Salt to taste
1 oz (28 grms) oil
½ teaspoon cummin powder
½ teaspoon ginger powder
¼ teaspoon turmeric
1/8 teaspoon dry mustard seed
1 tablespoon coriander leaves *or* watercress
   leaves *or* 2 teaspoons coriander powder
2 bay leaves

2 servings

Method

1. Chop onion and garlic. Cut up the tomatoes.
2. Boil lentils and tomatoes in a saucepan, with water to cover, and salt, till the lentils are really soft.
3. Heat the oil in a large frying pan.
4. Then add onions and garlic and fry till they are golden.
5. Then add ginger, turmeric, cummin, mustard seed and coriander powder, if used, and fry very gently for five minutes.
6. Put in the lentil and tomato mixture, the bay leaves or watercress leaves (if used).
7. Boil for one minute. Serve hot with rice.

Source: adapted from recipe in "Cooking the Indian Way" by Attia Hosain and Sita Pasricha.
Reproduced by permission of The Hamlyn Publishing Group Limited

See also Cape Kedgeree, South Africa, for a very simple Indian vegetarian dish.

Bhurta

Ingredients

400 grms or about 1 lb aubergines
100 grms or about 4 oz tomatoes
100 grms or about 4 oz peas
1 cup natural yoghurt
50 grms or about 2 oz onions
35-50 grms (1-2 oz) butter or soya bean oil
2 cloves garlic
Seeds from 1 cardamom pod
Pinch cinnamon
1 clove
Pinch cummin seed
Salt and pepper to taste

3 servings

Method

1. Boil aubergines for about 10 minutes and take off their skin.
2. Boil the peas in salted water for about 5 minutes.
3. Fry thinly sliced onions and spices.
4. Add skimmed tomatoes and boiled aubergines and cook for 15 minutes mashing the aubergines and mixing all the ingredients very well together.
5. Add beaten yoghurt and cook until the food is almost dry.
6. Add the cooked peas, and serve very hot, garnished with slices of hard boiled egg.

Source: India House, Aldwych, London.

Non-vegetarian dishes

Biryani

Ingredients

Spices for marinade mixture

½ teaspoon ground cinnamon
½ teaspoon ground cloves
½ teaspoon ground cardamom seeds
½ teaspoon chilli powder
1 small carton plain yoghurt
1 teaspoon turmeric powder
1 teaspoon cummin
1 teaspoon garlic powder or
1 garlic clove — crushed

1 lb (450 grms) lean meat (e.g. lamb or chicken)
  cubed
1 onion sliced

8 oz (225 grms) Patna or Basmati rice
Oil or ghee for frying
Salt to taste
Water to cook rice

about 4 servings

Method

1. Mix together all the spices and yoghurt.
2. Add cubed meat to this mixture.
3. Marinade for at least 3 hours.
4. Wash the rice and leave to soak for
   30 minutes.
5. Parboil rice and drain.
6. Fry onions until golden brown.
7. Place two-thirds of rice in a heavy pan and
   cover with fried onions and meat.
8. Cover fried onions and meat with remaining
   rice.
9. Make a few holes with fork or spoon handle
   to allow steam to rise.
10. Make sure the pan is completely air-tight by
    putting foil under the lid.
11. Cook on a very low heat or in a cool oven
    (300°F — Gas Mark 2) for about 2 hours.

Source: Community Education Trust

Chicken kurma

Ingredients

Half a chicken chopped into pieces about
  1 ½ inches (4 cm) in diameter*
1 inch (3 cm) cube of creamed coconut
6-10 sprigs of green coriander (or watercress or
  parsley)
2-5 cloves garlic, crushed (use more or less
  according to taste)
1 inch (3 cm) cube of peeled root ginger (grated
  or crushed)
2 medium onions chopped
4 peeled pods of cardamom
2 inch (5 cm) stick of cinnamon
4 cloves
1 teaspoon turmeric powder
1-2 green chillies (optional)
2 teaspoons coriander powder (or more if no
  green coriander is available)
1 ¼ teaspoons paprika powder
2 tablespoons lemon juice
Oil
Water
Salt to taste (about ½ teaspoon)
4 servings

Method

1. Put oil into a large thick-based saucepan and
   heat.
2. Add onions and fry until golden brown.
3. Add crushed ginger and garlic. Stir and fry for
   about 2 minutes.
4. Add finely chopped green coriander.
5. Cut chillies in half and add to the mixture.
   Fry for a further 2 minutes.
6. Make turmeric, coriander powder, and paprika
   powder into a thick rich paste with water.
7. Add to the mixture.
8. Stirring continuously, fry for 3-4 minutes.
9. Add cinnamon, cardamom, and cloves, and
   stir well.
10. When all the spices are well coated with oil,
    add a cup of water, the creamed coconut and
    salt to taste.
11. When the coconut has melted, add the
    chicken pieces, stir until the mixture boils,
    cover and simmer slowly until the mixture is
    cooked.(The curry can be cooked quickly in a
    pressure cooker.)
12. Add lemon juice and serve with rice and
    pappadoms.

* It is also possible to cut the chicken after
cooking.
NB:
1. The water and lemon juice can be replaced by
   2 small cartons of natural yoghurt.
2. This is a typical South Indian curry. In parts of
   North India, it is made with soaked and
   crushed poppy seed instead of coconut.

Source: Jacquie Watson

43

Nargisi kofta

Ingredients

8 oz (225 grms) minced beef or mutton
2 hard-boiled eggs
3 slices bread
Oil for frying

Spices

1 tablespoon onion, very finely chopped or ground
1 teaspoon garlic, peeled, sliced or ground
½ teaspoon chilli powder
1 teaspoon coriander powder
¼ inch (1 cm) root ginger, peeled and grated
¼ teaspoon garam masala
2 bay leaves
1 tablespoon yoghurt
Salt to taste
2 glacé cherries for decoration

Method

1. Soak the bread in the water and crumble into the minced meat.
2. Add a little salt and mix well.
3. Heat some oil and fry the mixture till the mince changes colour.
4. Remove from the flame and when sufficiently cool, shape meat mixture around eggs until the eggs are fully covered.
5. Cut the koftas lengthwise and keep aside.
6. Heat 2 tablespoons oil and add the remaining ingredients, constantly stirring until the strong smell of spices disappears.
7. Add a little water to make up a thick gravy.
8. Place the koftas in the bubbling gravy, egg side up.
9. After 5 minutes remove from flame and decorate each kofta with half a cherry before serving.

Source: Rebecca Young

Royal chops

Ingredients

1 lb (450 grms) lamb chops
5 tablespoons oil
1 large onion finely sliced
A drop of saffron colouring dissolved in water (called Kesari rang)

Spices

1 teaspoon of mixed root ginger and garlic clove, pounded finely
1 teaspoon powdered coriander seeds
½ teaspoon chilli powder
1 inch (3cm) cinnamon stick
2 cardamom seeds, peeled and ground
2 cloves
1 tablespoon yoghurt
Salt to taste

Method

1. Peel and grate root ginger. Peel and slice or crush garlic. Mix to make one teaspoonful together.
2. Put the spices into the yoghurt. Marinade the chops in this mixture for half an hour.
3. Heat the oil in the pan and fry the onions until they are soft and light brown.
4. Then add the marinaded meat and spices and salt and keep frying, constantly turning with a spoon to stop it from sticking to the bottom. Add a little water if the spices tend to stick.
5. When droplets of oil separate from the spices, add just enough water to tenderise the meat.
6. When the meat is tender, add the saffron colouring and allow to simmer for two more minutes.

Source: Rebecca Young

Lamb curry

Ingredients

1 lb (450 grms) lean lamb, cubed
2 green chillies, chopped, or 1 teaspoon chilli
  powder
2 onions thinly sliced
1 garlic clove crushed
1 large tomato or half tin tomatoes, drained
½ teaspoon turmeric powder
1 teaspoon coriander powder
1 teaspoon garam masala
¼ teaspoon ground cloves
1 teaspoon cummin powder
¼ teaspoon ground cinnamon
Sprig mint leaves, chopped
Sprig coriander leaves (if available) chopped
2 small cartons yoghurt
Salt to taste
Oil or ghee for frying
Stock to use if curry becomes too dry

About 4 servings

Method

1. Heat oil or ghee.
2. Fry onion, garlic and green chillies for a few
   minutes on gentle heat.
3. Add the lamb and fry for about 10 minutes.
4. Add the tomatoes and cook for a further 10-15
   minutes on low heat.
5. Add the spices, herbs and yoghurt.
6. Cook uncovered on moderate heat until meat
   is cooked and the yoghurt evaporated.
7. If juices evaporate before meat is cooked, or a
   moister curry is required, add stock made with
   chicken cube, according to requirements.

Source: Community Education Trust

Snacks & side dishes

Samosas

Ingredients for the pastry

1 lb (450 grms) plain flour
½ teaspoon baking powder
1 teaspoon salt
1 oz (28 grms) melted butter or ghee
4 tablespoons yoghurt

and for the filling

1 medium-sized onion, chopped
2 cloves garlic, very finely chopped or crushed
1 oz (28 grms) butter or ghee
12 oz (336 grms) minced meat
2 teaspoons coriander powder
½ teaspoon ginger powder
½ teaspoon chilli powder
1 teaspoon garam masala
salt to taste

Method

1. Sieve the flour, baking powder and salt into a
   bowl.
2. Add 1 oz (28 grms) melted butter or ghee and
   the yoghurt and make into a pliable dough.
   Knead thoroughly so that the dough is
   smooth.
3. Set on one side.
4. Heat 1 oz (28 grms) butter or ghee and in it fry
   the onion and garlic till golden.
5. Add the mince, spices and salt and fry for
   about 5 minutes.
6. Cover and cook over gentle heat till the meat is
   cooked.
7. Knead the dough again.
8. Take small walnut-sized pieces of dough and
   make into round balls.
9. Flatten and roll out on a floured board.
10. Make thin rounds the size of a saucer.
11. Cut in half.
12. Make into a cone, seal with water and fill with
    the meat mixture.
13. Wet open edges with water and press
    together.
14. When all the samosas are ready, fry in deep
    fat till they are crisp and golden.

Source: 'Cooking the Indian way'. by Attia Hosain and Sita
       Pasricha.
Reproduced by permission of The Hamlyn Publishing Group
Limited

Pakoras

Ingredients for the batter

1 ½ teaspoons turmeric
Pinch bicarbonate soda
1 teaspoon black onion seed
10 tablespoons gram flour (besan)
7-8 tablespoons water
1 ½ teaspoons finely grated ginger
Oil for deep frying
Pinch salt or less

Vegetables that can be frittered

Thinly sliced potatoes
Aubergines in ¼ '' (1 cm) rounds
Cauliflower florets
Spinach leaves
Chopped onions

Method

1. Sieve the besan, turmeric, bicarbonate of soda, black onion seed into a bowl.
2. Gradually add water and beat the mixture to a thick paste.
3. Heat oil till it is very hot.
4. Add 8 oz (224 grms) chopped onions or another vegetable to the batter and drop in teaspoonfuls into the oil.
5. Fry till the fritters are crisp.

Source: Lynn Teskey
 and 'Cooking the Indian way', by Attia Hosain and Sita Pasricha.
Reproduced by permission of The Hamlyn Publishing Group Limited

Mint or coriander leaf chutney

Ingredients

2 cups of mint or coriander leaves
1 green chilli
2 cloves garlic
1 teaspoon lime juice
Pinch brown sugar
Pinch Cayenne pepper
Few drops water if necessary

Method

1. Put all ingredients in the blender and crush until you have an even consistency.
2. Eat with pakoras or samosas.

Lynn Teskey

Tomato chutney

Ingredients

1 lb (448 grms) tomatoes
2 tablespoons sultanas
1 tablespoon lime juice
¾ tablespoon dark brown sugar
¾ teaspoon finely grated root ginger
A little cummin seed

Method

1. Peel and grate the ginger.
2. Heat a dry empty saucepan; when it is hot, put in the cummin seed and continue to heat the saucepan till you smell the rich scent of cummin roasting; let is roast but not burn and then remove it from the saucepan and grind it, with a pestle and mortar for instance.
3. Meanwhile soften the tomatoes by cooking them at boiling point for 5-8 minutes.
4. To the tomatoes add the sultanas, lime juice, sugar, ginger and finally the cummin.
5. Eat with pakoras or samosas.

Lynn Teskey

Puris

Deep fried bread

Ingredients

12 oz (336 grms) wholewheat flour
2 oz (56 grms) margarine or butter
Some lovage (optional)
Water

Method

1. Rub the margarine into the flour till the mixture is like fine breadcrumbs.
2. Boil ¼ pint water (0.2 litre) and mix some (but not all) of it with the fat and flour till you have a stiff dough. Add lovage if desired.
3. Break the dough into small lumps and roll them with a rolling pin into very thin pancakes about three inches or 8 cm in diameter. (Don't use any flour to roll them in.)
4. Take a one pint (half litre) thick bottomed saucepan and nearly fill it with cooking oil.
5. Heat the oil till it is so hot that a tiny piece of dough placed in it instantly rises to the surface.
6. Fry each puri individually for just a few seconds, removing it as soon as it has risen, using a slatted spoon.

Pushpa Knottenbelt Naik, Suresh Kumar

Raita

(Yoghurt and cucumber)

Ingredients

1 pint (.25 litre) plain yoghurt
½ cucumber, peeled and grated
½ knife-point of mustard
¼ teaspoonful salt
a sprinkling of Cayenne pepper
1/8 teaspoonful, preferably fresh, or if not powdered garlic

Method

Mix the ingredients and leave the mixture to stand in a cool place, for example a refrigerator.

This is very good with curry or hot dishes.

Source: Pushpa Knottenbelt Naik

Indonesia

Java, the cultural and political heart of the country, is very densely populated. The average farm size is only 0.3 hectare (0.75 acre). About 40% of Java's rural households own no farming land at all, and even a "large" farmer is only someone with more than 2 hectares of irrigated paddy fields. The refined and intricate irrigation system is already facing acute stresses, and has suffered from salting after hillsides are cleared.

Thanks to the Green Revolution, Indonesia's rice production has risen by about 40% in the last ten years, but production increases have been at the price of equity.

An Oxfam-supported project

Rearing small animals can be a very worthwhile and useful enterprise for peasant farming families with little or no land for crop growing on any scale. Oxfam has helped a number of communities in Indonesia in this way — providing funds for the purchase of rabbits, sheep, cows, and goats. Not only do the animals provide an extra source of protein, they provide a new and extra source of income too.

One of the schemes is run by the community development department of a large hospital in Yogyakarta, an evolution from their village nutritional and preventive health services. One hundred poor families in four villages have each been allocated four rabbits — 3 does and one buck 'on credit'. They repay their livestock loans in due course with the offspring, which in turn are given to other poor families — a revolving rabbit loan fund. The selected families participate in training sessions in their villages, learning about making hutches, feeding rabbits, and general care and maintenance.

As the rabbit numbers expand in the future, the families will be able to eat them or sell them.

Population	146,600,000
Area	1,919,000 sq. km.
	740,925 sq. miles
Arable land	19,500,000 hectares;
	48,184,500 acres
Life expectation	1960, 41 years; 1980, 53 years
Infant mortality	1960, 150 deaths;
	1980, 93 deaths
Population increase rate	2.3%
Labour force in agriculture	58%
Urbanisation	1960, 15%; 1980, 20%
Major city	Jakarta, the capital, 6.5 mn.
Food index	110%
Daily calorie supply per head	2,272 calories, 102%
Basic food crops	Rice, cassava, sweet potatoes, maize
Major export	Oil
Income per head	£182
Adult literacy	62%
Climate	Tropical

48

Main dishes always consist of rice and usually fish, and chicken or meat with vegetables. The Indonesian consommé, or 'soto' is very popular in all areas of Java and Madura, and in many cases it is consumed as a main dish, provided boiled or steamed rice is added.

A meat dish

Ingredients
22 oz. (616 grms) minced beef
2 oz. (56 grms) onion, fried in a little butter
3 full teaspoons boemboe rudjak (optional)
(or finely ground spices made up of chillies, lemongrass and garlic powder)
1 dessertspoon Chinese soy sauce
1 teaspoon ginger powder
$\frac{1}{4}$ teaspoon pepper
1 teaspoon salt
1 small piece of stem ginger in syrup per person; cut the pieces up very finely indeed

sauce
3 large sweet green peppers
Medium tin of tomatoes
1 dessertspoon Chinese soy sauce
1 dessertspoon tomato ketchup
2 teaspoons maize flour
Juice of half a lemon
A tin of bamboo shoots (optional)

8 servings

Method
1. Mix all the ingredients for the mince together thoroughly and fry them in hot oil until they are cooked.*
2. Then put the mixture in a casserole in the oven to keep warm.
3. Clean the frying pan.
4. Cut the green peppers into small thin pieces and fry in oil.
5. When they are cooked, add the tomatoes, soy sauce and tomato ketchup. Shake the pan from time to time.
6. Make a mixture of maize or other quick cooking flour and the juice of half a lemon.
7. Mix this into the sauce and put in a covered container.
8. Fry some bamboo shoots in butter until they are golden brown and serve them in the same dish with the mince covered with the sauce.

*You can also make the raw mince mixture into balls bound with 2 small eggs and rolled in bread-crumbs and then fry the balls.

Marijke Drayer-Poortman

Egg and tomato sambal

Ingredients
3 tomatoes
2 eggs
1 small onion
1 chilli, chopped
Salt
Pepper

2 servings

Method
1. Lightly fry onion.
2. Add sliced tomatoes and a chilli.
3. Break in the eggs and mix well. Add seasoning.
4. Cook for three minutes.

Source: Pot luck

Serikaya (Banana pudding)

Ingredients
3 eggs
1 cup of sugar
3 bananas
Powdered vanilla pod to taste (or essence)
1 cup of milk

Method
1. Beat the eggs with the vanilla, add the sugar and milk and stir the mixture.
2. Add the sliced bananas, pour into a basin or dish and steam gently for 30-40 minutes in a bain-marie till set.

Source: Pot luck

Sate kambing (Lamb Sate)

Ingredients for Sauce
called "Bumbu sate" in Java

4 oz. (112 grms) peanuts (or crunchy peanut butter)
2 shallots
1 clove garlic
Chilli powder to taste
Salt to taste
1 slice terasi (a dark coloured paste made from shrimps, usually obtainable in Chinese shops)
1 tablespoon lemon juice
1 teaspoon brown sugar
1 tablespoon vegetable or olive oil
1½ cups water

Meat
Lamb, chicken or beef can be used for this recipe. Allow about 4 oz (112 grms) per person and cut into small pieces.

Ingredients for marinade
2 shallots or half onion, sliced
1 clove garlic, crushed
2 tablespoons soy sauce
Pinch hot chilli powder
1 teaspoon ground coriander
1 teaspoon ground ginger
1 tablespoon lemon juice, or vinegar
2 tablespoons tamarind water
1 tablespoon olive or vegetable oil

Method
1. Make the marinade.
2. Leave the meat to stand in the marinade for at least two hours, and preferably overnight.
3. Make the sauce, (recipe below).
4. Then thread the meat onto skewers.
5. Grill the meat on one side for about 5-8 minutes.
6. Turn and grill meat again for 5-8 minutes; barbecuing will cook the meat more quickly.

Method to cook the sauce
1. Fry the peanuts in a little hot oil and grind to a powder, preferably in a liquidiser.
2. Crush the shallots, garlic and terasi.
3. Add chilli and salt.
4. Heat a little oil and fry shallots, garlic and terasi, chilli and salt.
5. Add water, and when it is boiling put in ground peanuts, lemon juice (or vinegar or tamarind) and sugar and stir well.
6. Continue boiling until the sauce is thick (about 3 minutes).
7. Pour the sauce on the meat and sprinkle with fried onion or serve the sauce as a dip.

NB: Brown or Basmati rice and green salad go well with this dish.

Source: Nicki Sissons.

Fish in ginger sauce

Ingredients
Fish: for example, 12 fish fingers; 4 pieces of cod

For white sauce
1 pint (0.6 litre) milk
1½ oz (42 grms) margarine
1½ oz (42 grms) flour
a little salt

For flavouring of sauce
Oil
1 garlic clove, chopped or crushed
2 onions finely chopped
1 inch (3 cm) root ginger peeled and grated
Dash of chilli sauce
Juice of half a lemon
½ teaspoon brown sugar
1 dessertspoon soy sauce
a little syrup from a bottle of stem ginger (optional)

4 servings

Method
1. Fry or grill the fish and set aside.
2. Make a white sauce. Cook it and set aside.
3. Take a thick-bottomed frying pan and heat the cooking oil till it is very hot.
4. Put in the onions and garlic and fry gently till they are golden coloured.
5. Pour the white sauce into the frying pan and add the grated root ginger and all the other ingredients.
6. Add a little more or a little less according to taste.
7. Pour the sauce over the fish and serve.

Marijke Drayer-Poortman

Sate ajam (Grilled chicken)

Ingredients
1 large chicken
Black pepper
Salt
Chinese soy sauce

Sauce
1 steamed red chilli
2–3 cloves garlic
4 tablespoons peanut butter
Meat cube dissolved in a little water
Lemon juice

6–8 servings

Method
1. Cut chicken into small pieces and stick these on metal skewers.
2. Mix some ground black pepper, salt and a sprinkling of Chinese soy sauce.
3. Pour this over the chicken and cook until tender.
4. Grill brown just before serving.
5. Serve on skewers, accompanied by a sauce made as follows: —
6. Mince or pound together one steamed red chilli and two or three cloves of fried garlic.
7. Mix this with the peanut butter, and a meat cube dissolved in a little boiling water.
8. Add lemon juice to taste.

Source: 'Pot Luck'.

Soto ajam (Chicken bouillon)

Ingredients
1 large chicken
Oil for frying
Ground ginger to taste
2 potatoes
1 or 2 sticks of celery
Onions and garlic to taste
Salt and pepper
2 eggs
2 cooked carrots
1 to 2 cooked leeks

6–8 servings

Method
1. Cook the carrots and leeks.
2. Reserve the stock.
3. Cut up the chicken.
4. Fry the onions, garlic and ginger without browning.
5. Boil the chicken with the onions and garlic in the stock till the chicken is tender.
6. Hard boil the eggs and slice them.
7. Cut the cooked carrots into small pieces.
8. Slice the uncooked celery and cooked leeks finely.
9. To serve: put in each bouillon cup a spoonful of chicken meat cut up small, a few slices of egg, some fried potato, onion and garlic, carrot, celery and leek. Pour hot chicken broth into every cup, and serve hot.

Source: 'Pot Luck'.

Jordan

Much of the total area is desert and the population is predominantly concentrated in the capital of Amman, half a dozen other major towns, and for the most part widely scattered through rural areas in the western half of the country. In the June 1967 war, Jordan lost Jerusalem, the main tourist attraction, and much of the population living on the West Bank. There are thought to be at least an extra 250,000 refugees for the government and international organisations to care for.

An Oxfam-supported project in Jordan

Oxfam has made several grants in Jordan to enable women to undertake vocational training while their children are properly supervised.

One such project is in the village of Ghor Mazra'a in the remote and hot area on the shores of the Dead Sea. The village has about 3000 people, of Bedouin and slave origin, who eke out a living by subsistence farming, some shepherding or (if they are landless) working on the fields of other people. More than half the farm land is unused because of low rainfall and the high cost of irrigation.

A high government priority is the development of socio-economic facilities that will stem the migration from rural areas of Jordan to the cities. It is felt that a child care centre is one of many services that can be offered to encourage the development of alternative income-generating sources, women's training courses and the promotion of improved family welfare.

But many of the women at Ghor Mazra'a,who have to undergo many closely spaced pregnancies and have very limited horizons, work in the fields, either those of their own families or those of bigger landowners. Children are left with people who are too old to work, and who may be unable to supervise them properly.

In 1982 Oxfam gave £3,763 to provide equipment for a child care centre at Ghor Mazra'a, where the children will be safe and secure, well fed and given an opportunity to grow into healthy, socially adjusted adults. As a result, the mothers will be more inclined to take advantage of newly established work and educational opportunities. These women are more likely to become involved in the management of their lives and to add to the welfare of their entire family.

Population	3.2 million
Area	98,000 sq. km. 37,837 sq. miles
Arable land	1,380,000 hectares
	3,409,000 acres
Life expectation	1960, 47 years; 1980, 61 years
Infant mortality	1960, 136 deaths;
	1980, 69 deaths
Population increase rate	3.4%
Labour force in agriculture	25%
Urbanisation	1960, 43%; 1980, 56%
Big town	Amman, the capital, 1.18 mn.
Food index	89%
Daily calorie supply per head	2107 calories, 62%
Basic food crops	Wheat, barley
Major export	Phosphates
Income per head	£604
Adult literacy	70%
Climate	Hot and dry summers, cool winters

Labna

Ingredients
Yoghurt
Salt
Olive oil
Paprika powder

Method

1. Add ½ to 1 teaspoon salt per pint (or half litre) of yoghurt, according to taste.
2. Pour the yoghurt into a sieve or colander lined with damp muslin or fine cotton cloth.
3. Allow the yoghurt to drain overnight, or tie the corners of the cloth together and hang the bundle over a bowl or the sink. The whey will drain away leaving a very light, soft, creamy white curd cheese.
4. Shape this cheese into little balls.
5. Sprinkle the balls with olive oil and a little paprika powder, or roll them in it.

Source: *'A book of Middle Eastern food,' by Claudia Roden published by Penguins.*

Kampuchea

Population	6.9 million
Area	181,000 sq. km.
	69,000 sq. miles
Arable land	3,046,000 hectares
	7,526,600 acres
Life expectation	1960, 46 years;
	1980, Not known
Infant mortality	1960, 146 deaths;
	1980, Not known
Population increase rate	- 0.2%
Labour force in agriculture	73%
Urbanisation	1960, 11%; 1980, Not known
Big city	Phnom Penh, the capital, about 500,000
Food index	41%
Daily calorie supply per head	1926 calories, 78%
Basic food crop	Rice
Major exports	Rubber, kapok, gems
Income per head	Not known
Adult literacy	Not known
Climate	Tropical

'As we flew into Kampuchea in the early days of the relief operation in 1979, the landscape South and East of Phnom Penh reminded me of the surface of the moon', wrote Oxfam's Disasters Officer. 'In Kampuchea the craters mark the spots where thousands of tons of bombs fell from American planes on to suspected communist positions. They fell also on villages and farms, houses and roads, adults and children'.

Following the American bombing from 1970 to 1975, the victorious Khmer Rouge attempted to transform Kampuchea into an ideal Communist society which ended up with the deaths of an estimated 2 million people.

In 1979, the Vietnamese army intervened, driving the infamous Pol Pot and his followers out of power. Pol Pot left behind a country ravaged by war and revolution. Since that time the Kampuchean people have been striving to rebuild their country and civilisation. Oxfam began in 1979 to carry out our largest emergency relief programme ever involving £22 million over three years in agricultural development, rural water supplies, transport and communication, recon- struction of industry and social welfare pro- grammes. Although average rice yields are still barely 1 tonne per hectare, the availability of arable land and the low concentration of population has meant that the country is now nearly self- sufficient in food. Slowly, after more than a decade of destruction and turmoil, life in Kampuchea is slowly returning to normal. As a result of this recovery, a 'baby boom' has been taking place giving Kampuchea the highest birth rate in the world at present.

An Oxfam-supported project

Vegetables play a very important part in the diet and cuisine of south east Asia, and so vegetable seeds figured prominently in the first requests for emergency assistance with agriculture from Kampuchea in 1979. Half a ton of Chinese cabbage seed went in with the first barge-load of supplies from Singapore, to be followed by radish, cabbage, caulifilower and several types of beans. In the first three months the Oxfam-led consortium purchased and shipped in more than 40 tonnes of vegetable seeds.

For the Kampuchean people, malnourished and weak after the horrors of the Pol Pot regime, vegetables had an important role to play in pro- viding vitamins, minerals and roughage in the diet. They could be grown easily too, by women and children on small plots of land — all important in the tragic situation where so many of the men had been killed.

The following year a further 14 tonnes of vegetable seeds were procured, giving a wider range including onions, green peppers, and turnips. These were provided for programmes in two provinces where there were still serious food shortages.

By Spring 1983, Oxfam had raised and spent altogether £22 million on aid and development in Kampuchea since the beginning of the emergency.

Royal rice

Ingredients

2 chicken legs, uncooked
8 oz. (250 grms) lean pork
4 prawns, shelled and deveined
4-6 cloves garlic, chopped
20 spring onions, chopped
6 oz. (185 grms) lard or fat
1 lb. (500 grms) cooked rice
Pinch fennel seed or a few fennel sprigs
2 tablespoons vinegar
Just over half pint (300 ml) medium white sauce
½ teaspoon Chinese five-spice essence
3 level tablespoons caster sugar
Dash of salt
Dash of pepper
2 eggs lightly beaten
2 level tablespoons pimiento strips
Fennel
Juice of 1 lemon

Serves 4 people

Method

1. Wash chicken, pork and prawns, and then dice.
2. Brown garlic and spring onions in fat in a large sauté pan.
3. Add diced meat and prawns, and sauté until flavour is nicely blended.
   This will take about 30 minutes.
4. Add the rice to the mixture and blend well.
5. Add pinch of fennel, vinegar, white sauce, five-spice essence, sugar, salt and pepper.
6. Heat for a few minutes to blend flavours.
7. Pour eggs into a greased pan, making a thin layer.
8. Heat until almost firm, then turn over.
9. Remove from heat, cut into very thin strips, and add to the rice mixture.
10. Place rice mixture in a serving dish and garnish with the pimiento strips and additional fennel.
11. Sprinkle with lemon juice.

Note:
Chinese five-spice essence, which consists of finely ground cloves, star anise, cinnamon, fennel and liquorice root, can be bought in shops specialising in Chinese food.

Source: "The Cookbook of the United Nations",
by Barbara Kraus

Kenya

There have been revolutionary changes in land tenure and farming patterns in Kenya in the last 20 years. Private land ownership has developed in central tribal areas.

Large tracts of the so-called former "White High-lands" have been transferred from European to African private ownership.

Peasant farmers have started growing tea, sugar, sisal, pyrethrum, coffee and wattle bark which previously were grown on plantations.

Inequality of land holdings is particularly marked in Kenya. Open unemployment is a serious problem, especially in urban areas, to which land-less and landpoor people move searching for work.

The "working poor" who work long hours for little return are not much better off than the unemployed and are far more numerous.

An Oxfam-supported project in Kenya
Ekarakara, a parish with 50,000 people, lies in a semi-arid part of Kenya where famine has been known for many years. The area is densely popu-lated, although it was settled fairly recently.

When Father Fonseca, the Roman Catholic priest of this parish, came to Ekarakara, he found that very many families lived from hand to mouth and did not have the money to buy tools that were needed to work on their small farms. Some people wanted to manure their land but had no wheel-barrows to carry the dung from the cattle enclosures to the plots. Government Agricultural Services were very underdeveloped.

Father Fonseca found that only 10% of house-holds had a toilet. But health workers started visiting homes to advise people to dig latrines and 60 self-help work groups were started. Some work groups started digging latrines but did not have picks and shovels to get the job done quickly.

Father Fonseca applied to and obtained from Oxfam £7,852 to buy the hoes, shovels and wheelbarrows that were needed for this work. They were given to individual farmers and to work groups, a very large number of whose members are women.

Population	15.9 million
Area	583,000 sq. km.
	225,000 sq. miles
Arable land	2,275,000 hectares
	5,621,000 acres
Life expectation	1960, 41 years; 1980, 55 years
Infant mortality	1960, 138 deaths;
	1980, 87 deaths
Population increase rate	3.4%
Labour force in agriculture	77%
Urbanisation	1960, 7%; 1980, 14%
Big city	Nairobi, the capital 828,000
Food index	86%
Daily calorie supply per head	2032 calories, 96%
Basic food crops	Maize, sorghum, wheat
Major exports	Oil, coffee
Income per head	£178
Adult literacy	About 50%
Climate	Tropical on coast. Semi-temperate or temperate inland

Mahamri (Swahili buns)

Ingredients

500 grms (or about 1 lb) white flour
About 56 grms or 2 oz sugar
2 dessertspoonfuls ghee
1 teaspoon yeast diluted in a little warm water
1½ cups coconut milk or water
Oil for deep frying
½ teaspoon cardamom seeds or rose water

Method

1. Thoroughly knead the flour, sugar, cardamom seeds, ghee, coconut milk and yeast solution to form a dough.
2. Knead until the dough is smooth and blistered.
3. Divide into 8 balls.
4. Roll each ball into a six inch or 15cm circle.
5. Cut into quarters.
6. Put well apart on a floured board or paper and keep in a warm room for about two hours or until the dough has risen and becomes light.
7. Deep fry on both sides until brown. The buns should be a light, golden brown, but not dark brown.

   Serve hot with curry.

Source: Janet McCrae

NB:
This is the staple bread of Swahili people and some housewives make it every morning, for breakfast. It can be eaten cold or re-heated for dinner. It can be eaten with butter or alone.

Samaki wa kupaka

Ingredients

1 lb (450 grms) white whole fish, preferably seafish
Salt
Lemon juice

for sauce

1 fresh coconut (or dessicated coconut if unavailable)
warm water
2 medium onions, crushed or chopped finely
3 garlic cloves, crushed
2 tomatoes, chopped finely
1 teaspoon tomato purée
2 tablespoons lemon juice, or lime juice or 2 pods tamarind squeezed
Pinch chilli or Cayenne
Good shake of black pepper
Teaspoon salt
Pinch sage
Pinch caraway
1 teaspoon turmeric
1 teaspoon cinnamon
1 teaspoon
5 cardamom seeds (remove husks)

Method

1. Cut into the fish's flesh with a knife on each side and rub it with salt and lemon, lime or tamarind juice.
2. Make coconut milk by grating the coconut and squeezing it, with water, in a muslin bag several times.*
3. Pour boiling water over 2 teacups of dessicated coconut and place in a liquidiser, working in with more water.
4. After liquidising, pour into muslin bag and squeeze hard into a saucepan.
5. Add to the milk the rest of the ingredients.
6. Heat the mixture on a very slow heat stirring vigorously. If you don't do so the mixture will curdle.
7. The sauce should become thick and creamy and pink in colour with a slightly acid tang.
8. Soak the fish in the sauce and then put it under the grill, cooking on both sides.**
9. Serve with extra sauce and rice, cassava or maize porridge and a salad made of onion and tomato with lemon juice and salt dressing.

Source: Janet McCrae

* You can re-use the coconut in biscuits.
** In Kenya, the fish would be grilled very slowly on a charcoal fire.

Population	2.7 million
Area	10,000 sq. km., 3861 sq. miles
Arable land	348,000 hectares; 859,900 acres
Life expectation	1960, 58 years; 1980, 66 years
Infant mortality	1960, 68 deaths; 1980, 41 deaths
Population increase rate	0.7%
Labour force in agriculture	9%
Urbanisation	1960, 44%; 1980, 76%
Big city	Beirut, the capital, 1.5 mn.
Food index	83%
Daily calorie supply per head	2495 calories, 112%
Basic food crops	Wheat, potatoes
Major exports	Building materials, black cement, fruit, chemical products, aluminium products
Income per head	Not known
Adult literacy	Not known
Climate	Subtropical

58

Since 1975 the commercial and economic life of Lebanon has been overshadowed by violence and political uncertainty. No section of the economy has been spared. Although much of the cultivable land is marginal, Lebanon has traditionally been a food exporter to several Arab countries. But the war and subsequent outbreaks of fighting disrupted agricultural production in general. The violence has affected industry very badly too. The human suffering has been incalculable.

Oxfam-supported project in Lebanon

In 1982, during the battle for Tyre, 211 fishermen's families had their livelihood destroyed when heavy fighting smashed their boats and incinerated their nets. A survey under the direction of George Haddad costed the damage meticulously. The fishermen were politically "clean" and Oxfam made a grant for £11,037 to replace their nets so that they could go to sea again once curfew restrictions permitted. The Oxfam Field Director commented "Such a grant demonstrates clearly Oxfam's desire to support all parties in need, regardless of their origin".

Oxfam also gave £11,111 in 1982 to repair fishing boats at Sidon that were damaged during the fighting. The project was undertaken in co-operation with a local Islamic Cultural Centre and the Mayor of Sidon.

Kofta bil Sania
(Minced meat loaf in a tray)
Ingredients
2 lb. (900 grms) lamb, beef or veal, minced
2 onions, grated
Salt and black pepper
   1 teaspoon ground cinnamon or allspice
or 1 teaspoon ground cumin and
   1 teaspoon ground coriander
Oil or butter
2¼ oz (63 grms) tin tomato concentrate
4 tablespoons finely chopped parsley
½ pint (0.3 litre) water

6-8 servings

Method
1. Have the meat minced two or three times if possible.
2. Add the onions and work them together to a very smooth, soft paste.
3. Season to taste with salt, pepper and cinnamon or allspice (or the cumin and coriander), and mix these spices in thoroughly.
4. Spread the mixture evenly over the bottom of a large oiled or buttered baking tray, flattening it out with a wooden spoon. The meat should be ¾ to 1'' (about 25 mm) thick.
5. Dot with butter shavings and bake in a moderate oven (375°F or Mark 4) until the surface of the meat is browned and gives off a roasted aroma (about 40 minutes).
6. Mix the tomato concentrate with half a pint (0.3 litre) water and pour it over the meat.
7. Return the loaf to the oven and continue to bake for about 10 minutes, or until the tomato sauce has become absorbed and the meat is well cooked. It will shrink away from the sides of the tray.
8. Turn the loaf on to a large serving dish and cut into squares or lozenges; or if you are using a round baking tray, cut it into wedges like a cake.
9. Garnish with chopped parsley and serve with mashed or roast potatoes or a selection of salads.

Source: 'A book of Middle Eastern food', by Claudia Roden, published by Penguins.

Fattush (Bread salad)
Ingredients
1 pitta bread
1 cos lettuce coarsely chopped
1 cucumber peeled and coarsely chopped
3 medium tomatoes, coarsely chopped
1 small mild onion, finely chopped, or a bunch of spring onions finely chopped
Good bunch of parsley, finely chopped
Few sprigs of fresh mint, finely chopped, or 1 tablespoon dry mint

For the dressing
Juice of 1 lemon
5 tablespoons olive oil
1 clove garlic, crushed
Salt and pepper

Method
1. Open out the pitta bread and toast the thin halves under the grill or in the oven until crisp and brown.
2. Put the vegetables and herbs in a serving bowl.
3. Break the toast with your hands into small pieces over them.
4. Toss with the dressing just before serving.

Source: Claudia Roden

Mudardana
Ingredients
250 grms (8 oz) large brown lentils
250 grms (8 oz) Basmati rice
2 large onions cut into thick half moon slices
5-6 tablespoons oil
Salt and pepper

Method
1. Wash the lentils and cover with water in a pan.
2. Simmer without salt for 20 minutes or until tender.
3. Add the rice, washed, and enough water to make the liquor up to a little more than the volume of the rice.
4. Season with salt and pepper and cook covered until the rice is done, which will take about 20 minutes, adding water if the rice becomes too dry.
5. Fry the onions in hot oil, stirring constantly until they are very brown, almost caramelised.
6. Serve hot or cold in a flat dish with the onions and their cooking oil poured over the top.

Source: Claudia Roden

Malaysia

Population	13.9 million
Area	330,000 sq. km. 127,413 sq. miles
Arable land	4,310,000 hectares 10,650,000 acres
Life expectation	1960, 53 years; 1980, 64 years
Infant mortality	1960, 72 deaths; 1980, 31 deaths
Population increase rate	2.4%
Labour force in agriculture	47%
Urbanisation	1960, 25%; 1980, 29%
Big city	Kuala Lumpur, the capital, 454,000
Food index	116%
Daily calorie supply per head	2610 calories, 116%
Basic food crop	Rice
Major exports	Oil, rubber, palm oil products, logs
Income per head	£689
Adult literacy	Not known
Climate	Tropical

Malaysia is one of the wealthier developing countries and the standard of living has risen dramatically for many of her people over the last two or three decades. The agricultural sector remains the poorest, however, with the people dependent on rice farming at the bottom of the scale.

Malaysia's prosperity stems from the wide range of raw materials which she produces. Malaysia is one of the few developing countries that runs a 'trade surplus', i.e. she exports more than she imports.

An Oxfam-supported project

A Conference was held at Penang in Malaysia on Pesticides. Oxfam paid for people from Indonesia, Bangladesh and the Philippines to attend this conference, from which was launched the Pesticides Action Network International.

Curry lunch

Ingredients
1 chicken, 3½ lb. (approx. 1.75 kilo), cut in sections
2 medium onions, finely chopped
2 cloves of garlic, finely sliced
1 pint (about ½ litre) of water
Salt to taste
3 tablespoons vegetable oil
½ in. (13 mm.) slice creamed coconut
3 heaped tablespoons curry powder, made into a paste with water

Rice
2 teacups long-grain (Patna) rice
2 teaspoons salt
3 teacups of hot or cold water, to which 2 bouillon cubes have been added.
4–5 servings

Method
1. Put oil in large saucepan, and when hot, fry garlic and onions until soft.
2. Add the curry paste and fry a little longer.
3. Put in the chicken, mix well and fry for about five minutes.
4. Add water, creamed coconut, salt and stir well.
5. Bring to the boil, lower heat and simmer for two hours, or till chicken is cooked.

For the rice
1. Put rice in saucepan, and after washing, add the water and salt and bring to the boil quickly, uncovered.
2. When rice has absorbed most of the water, stir and cover.
3. Lower heat to simmer, and let the rice cook in its own steam.

Source: 'Pot Luck'.

Pork sweet and sour

Ingredients
12 oz (336 grms) pork fillet (or other lean cut)
Soy sauce
Vinegar
Flour
Salt, pepper
Olive oil
2 sweet green peppers
1 tin pineapple chunks or pieces
1 tin tomatoes
Brown sugar

Optional flavouring: pimiento, paprika
Optional side dishes or additions to the main dish: banana and/or nuts

Four servings

Method
1. Cut pork into half inch (1.5 cm) cubes and marinade overnight in a mixture of soy sauce and vinegar.
2. Drain pork, keeping the marinade, toss in mixture of flour, salt and pepper, and fry in olive oil. When cooked, set aside. (This operation can all be done in advance.)
3. Put the sliced green peppers into the pan and cook for 3-5 minutes.
4. Add the pineapple and the tomatoes, stir and heat through, adding the marinade and meat back into the mixture.
5. Finally stir in a little brown sugar if the pineapple has not provided sufficient sweetening.
6. If you would like to give a slightly hotter flavour, mix in half a diced pimiento chopped up very small, and sprinkle with paprika.
7. Serve immediately with rice.

Source: Elizabeth Stamp

What to serve with rice and curry:
Chutney
Pappadoms
Desiccated coconut, fried until nicely brown with no oil
Bananas, sliced
Pineapple cubes, seasoned with lemon juice
Salted peanuts
Sliced onion, seasoned with salt, vinegar and sugar
Sliced cucumber, seasoned with salt, vinegar and sugar
Tomatoes, diced and seasoned with lemon juice, salt and sugar

Mexico

After the Spanish conquered the country in the 16th century, the native Amerindians were forced by whites and people of mixed race to live in remote areas. Forests were cut down to make way for mining and cities. The result has been denudation of the land and subsequent erosion.

After a revolution in 1919, large estates were divided up, but now these little patches of land cannot support the tiller and the number of land-less peasants has exploded from 1.5m in 1950 to over 14m in 1980.

Mexico has for the last 50 years been growing vegetables and fruit for export rather than maize, which is less profitable, for home consumption. Mexico is a traditional area of major agribusiness investment.

An Oxfam-supported project in Mexico

Most people in the State of Chiapas are poor peasants, but a minority of Spanish-speaking landowners are rich and powerful. There are increasing numbers of landless people.

Chiapas is one of the most important oil-producing regions of Mexico. Three major hydro-electric power schemes are being built there and the State has recently become a major grain supplier to the rest of the country as well as a sugar cane producer.

Desmi, a local voluntary agency, has been working with groups of poor peasants in Chiapas for a number of years. This agency provides training for these communities' needs and when the communities choose to adopt some project, it supports them. Recently it has extended its work to assist women to participate more fully and effectively in the life of their own communities and the country in general.

The agency has a revolving loan fund which enables the communities to participate in economically productive projects (for example, bee-keeping, chicken and pig schemes).

After prolonged and supportive contact the peasant groups are now organising themselves to further their own interests.

Oxfam, which has been assisting the group since 1978, gave £10,410 in 1982.

Since Chiapas borders on Guatemala, many refugees have come there fleeing violence in their own country. In 1982, Oxfam gave £10,819 to assist the settlement of 130 Guatemalan refugee families in the jungle regions of Eastern Chiapas.

Population	69,800,000
Area	1,973,000 sq. km.
	761,000 sq. miles
Arable land	23,330,000 hectares
	57,648,430 acres
Life expectation	1960, 58 years; 1980, 65 years
Infant mortality	1960, 91 deaths;
	1980, 56 deaths
Population increase rate	3.1%
Labour force in agriculture	35%
Urbanisation	1960, 51%; 1980, 67%
Big city	Mexico City, the capital,
	14.4 million
Food index	103%
Daily calorie supply per head	2654 calories, 113%
Basic food crops	Maize, sorghum, wheat
Major export	Oil
Income per head	£889
Adult literacy	About 81%
Climate	Tropical in South. Temperate in highlands

Orange candy

Ingredients

3 cups sugar
1½ cups milk, scalded
2 grated orange rinds
Pinch salt
½ cup butter
1 cup chopped nuts

Method

1. Melt 1 cup sugar in a large saucepan, till the sugar is a rich yellow colour.
2. Then add milk slowly, stirring constantly.
3. Add remaining sugar and stir till it is dissolved.
4. Cook slowly without stirring till a very little of the mixture forms a firm ball in cold water.
5. Add grated orange rind, salt, butter and nuts.
6. Beat till it is creamy.
7. Pour into shallow oiled pan and mark into squares.

Source: 'Cookbook'. Recipes collected by the American Women's Literary Club, Lima.

Ceviche (Marinaded fish)

Ingredients

2 lb. (900 grms) filleted fish (raw haddock or any thickish white fish would do).
2 large onions
½ cup oil
1 cup lemon juice (PLJ for instance)
1 lb. (450 grms) tomatoes
2 bay leaves, ground
Half a small bottle of olives and capers
1 teaspoon chilli powder
1 cup white wine

6–7 servings

Method

1. Cut the fish into small pieces.
2. Soak it in the lemon juice with salt for 4 hours.
3. Drain.
4. Mix with other ingredients, leaving the olives whole.
5. Serve with salted crackers.

Source: 'Pot Luck'.

Mexican bread pudding

Ingredients

8 oz (224 grms) stale white bread
8 oz (224 grms) brown sugar
3 oz (84 grms) cooking cheese, grated
6 oz (168 grms) lard
3 oz (84 grms) butter
1 stick cinnamon
2 oz (56 grms) nuts (pinenuts or peanuts for instance)

Method

1. Slice the bread and fry in the lard.
2. Put the brown sugar and cinnamon in half a cup of water and let it simmer for 3 minutes.
3. Grease a baking dish with butter and put a layer of bread slices, another of syrup, grated cheese, bits of butter and nuts, and so on until finished.
4. Put in the oven to brown and serve hot.

Source: Laura Beauregard Rodriguez de la Serna

This recipe is one of the most popular in Mexico.

Population	20.2 million
Area	447,000 sq. km.
	172,586 sq. miles
Arable land	7,719,000 hectares
	19,073,649 acres
Life expectation	1960, 47 years; 1980, 56 years
Infant mortality	1960, 161 deaths;
	1980, 107 deaths
Population increase rate	3%
Labour force in agriculture	50%
Urbanisation	1960, 29%; 1980, 41%
Big city	Casablanca, the capital, 2.3 mn.
Food index	87%
Daily calorie supply per head	2534 calories, 107%
Basic food crops	Barley, wheat
Major export	Phosphates
Income per head	£382
Adult literacy	About 28%
Climate	Warm on the coast, hot inland

Modern large-scale farms, once owned mainly by European settlers, occupy just under 1 million hectares. These large farms produce about a quarter of the gross value of all crops including 80% of the wine and citrus, a third of the vegetables and 15% of the cereals. The peasant farmers are less prosperous. Under an agricultural investment code, introduced in 1969, farmers in irrigated areas have to meet minimum standards of efficiency or they may be evicted. Farms of less than 5 hectares are no longer permitted on irrigated land.

Since independence, the growth in agricultural output has slowed and for some years has not kept pace with the growth in population. Morocco, once an exporter of wheat, has now become a heavy importer.

An Oxfam-supported project in Morocco
Oxfam's most recent grant was continued help with running costs for infant nutrition centres in Casablanca and Marrakesh in 1974/5.

Vegetable Couscous

Couscous is a type of hard wheat semolina which is steamed over a rich soup. Its name is derived from the sound that the steam makes as it pushes through the holes of the steamer.

This national dish of North African countries has as many versions as there are families. Though the soup may include meats of all kinds and fish, it is very good made with vegetables alone. You can use one, two, three, or as many as eight or nine fresh or dry vegetables. The art lies in throwing the vegetables in the pot according to the length of cooking time they need.

These days the only couscous available in this country is a pre-cooked variety which requires nothing but the addition of an equal volume of water and heating up over steam, or equally successfully, in a saucepan or the oven, in which case you will not need the traditional steamer called a 'couscousier'. The pre-cooked grain is easy to use but of course not as good as one cooked below over steam. Use as many vegetables as you like listed below.

Ingredients
for the soup

4oz-8oz (112 grms-225 grms) chickpeas soaked overnight
Half small white cabbage, shredded
1 large onion, chopped
8 oz (225 grms) turnips, peeled and cut in four
1 lb (450 grms) carrots, peeled and cut in four lengthwise
4 tomatoes, peeled and quartered
1 aubergine cut into cubes
1 lb (450 grms) pumpkin, peeled and seeded and cut into cubes (optional)
3 courgettes sliced
Bunch fresh coriander or parsley, chopped
2-3 tablespoons raisins or sultanas
3-4 cloves
1-2 teaspoons cinnamon
½ teaspoon ginger
2 teaspoons paprika
Salt
Good pinch Cayenne or chilli pepper (optional)

for the couscous

1 lb (about half a kg) couscous
1 tablespoon butter or oil

Method

1. Half fill a large saucepan with water.
2. Add the chickpeas, cabbage, onion, turnips, carrots, tomatoes and spices (but not the salt so that the chickpeas soften more quickly).
3. Bring to the boil, then simmer, covered, for 45 minutes.
4. Add the rest of the ingredients, taste and adjust the flavouring and cook for about another 30 minutes until the vegetables are done.
5. As soon as you have put this in, start preparing the couscous.
6. Put it in a bowl, sprinkle with a little salt and add the same volume (about ¾ pint or .32 litre) lukewarm water.
7. Stir well and let the grain swell for 15 minutes.
8. Then heat it up either by steaming it over the soup or in a saucepan over a low flame.
9. Add butter and stir it in.
10. Serve in soup bowls with the vegetables on top and plenty of broth poured over it.

Source: Claudia Roden

Two salads

Orange salad

1. Peel 3 large oranges, taking care to remove all the bitter white pith.
2. Slice very thinly and arrange on a plate.
3. Sprinkle with orange blossom water and dust lightly with ground cinnamon.

Orange and radish salad

1. Slice a bunch of radishes thinly.
2. Peel, slice and divide into small pieces one or two oranges.
3. Season lightly with salt and a little lemon juice.

Source: "A Book of Middle Eastern Food" by Claudia Roden

Mozambique

When independence was achieved from the Portuguese in 1975, the new Mozambique government inherited an economy ravaged by a drawn-out war and depleted of trained people. Nearly all the Portuguese left the country as independence approached, deserting and in some cases sabotaging the factories, farms and shops they left behind. The situation was exacerbated in the following years by the effect of Zimbabwe's war of liberation — the loss of earnings from transit traffic passing through Mozambique from the coast, and the direct effects of strikes by the Rhodesian air force up to 1979.

The new Mozambique government's reaction to these problems has been widespread nationalisation and an attempt to create a planned economy.

Population	12.1 million
Area	802,000 sq. km. 309,600 sq. miles
Arable land	3 mn. hectares; 7.6 mn. acres
Life expectation	1960, 37 years; 1980, 47 years
Infant mortality	1960, 160 deaths; 1980, 115 deaths
Population increase rate	4%
Labour force in agriculture	63%
Urbanisation	1960, 4%; 1980, 9%
Big city	Maputo, the capital, 850,000 people
Food index	75%
Daily calorie supply per head	1906 calories, 78%
Chief basic food crops	Maize, sorghum, cassava
Major exports	Cashew nuts, seafood, cement and concrete
Income per head	£97
Adult literacy	28%
Climate	Tropical

Four different sectors co-exist in the agricultural system. There are small family-owned farms, growing several crops. There are private plantations which each grow one crop, for example sugar, sisal and coconuts. There are state-owned plantations, each growing only one crop. Finally there is a co-operative sector, consisting of communal villages growing mixed crops such as maize, beans, potatoes. The government aims to create a system of state farms in each of the provinces and to convert the traditional sector into co-operatives.

Mozambique is in a state of growing political confrontation with South Africa and the South African-backed Mozambique Resistance Movement has been effectively disrupting the economy in the central provinces as well as hindering the strengthening of national trade and transit links.

Oxfam's aid to Mozambique

Oxfam makes an annual grant to the International Voluntary Service field worker in Mozambique. In 1982 Oxfam made a grant to the Mozambique Red Cross following a very serious drought.

Avocado salad

for 8 small side salads

Ingredients

1 head iceberg lettuce
2 tomatoes
2 avocados

Lemon dressing

1 cup bottled lemon juice
1 cup olive oil
1 cup peach or other fruit syrup
1 teaspoon salt
1 teaspoon salad herbs
¼ teaspoon pepper

Method

1. Arrange one piece of lettuce on each salad plate.
2. Alternate eight inch (20 cm) slices of tomato overlapping with avocados cut in thin uniform slices across the lettuce in a straight line.
3. Spoon two tablespoons of the lemon dressing over the avocado salad.

Source: ''The African Cookbook'' by Bea Sandler

Barbecued chicken

for 8 half chickens

Ingredients

1 teaspoon Cayenne pepper
1 tablespoon salt
1 teaspoon garlic powder
½ teaspoon ground ginger
1 teaspoon paprika
Half cup salad oil
4 × 2½ lb (1.1 kg) chickens

Method

1. Mix Cayenne pepper, salt, garlic powder, ground ginger, paprika and oil thoroughly.
2. Rub the whole chickens with the seasoned oil thoroughly on all sides.
3. Roast, boil or barbecue the chickens in your favourite manner, basting them from time to time with the seasoned oil till the chickens are done.
4. Cut chickens in half.
5. Serve with white rice.

Source: ''The African Cookbook'' by Bea Sandler

Nepal

The Himalayan kingdom of Nepal is a mountainous landlocked country. For centuries the foothills of the Himalayas were forested. Then, as man moved into these areas, small plots were cleared for food growing. More recently, trees have been felled on an ever-increasing scale for commercial timber and for fuel wood. Deforestation has reached alarming proportions in the last few years as the rising price of oil has forced millions of poor city dwellers to give up their kerosene cooking stoves and return to the burning of wood. Kathmandu has drawn on supplies of fuelwood from further and further afield.

Tree cutting has stripped the mountain slopes, causing widespread erosion, which in turn affects the water-holding capacity of the land and hence the agricultural output. Fewer trees attract less rain, and there is more frequent flooding in the plains of North India and Bangladesh as the melting snows pour unhindered down the barren mountain slopes into swollen rivers.

Oxfam-supported projects

The Nepal government has taken various measures to stop further timber cutting and promote reforestation. In one of the last primary hardwood regions of Nepal, all tree felling has been prohibited.

Tragically, the firewood fellers and carriers have found their livelihood suddenly banned. Oxfam has given money to cover the cost of a 3-year village development programme to help 3 villages whose people relied heavily on firewood cutting and carrying for their livelihood.

In another part of the country, at a gorge about 11 metres across and 3-4 metres deep, villagers had previously built an earthen dam and canal to irrigate their fields. But this dam was washed away during the monsoon. Oxfam has given money to cover the cost of cement and skilled labour to build a permanent irrigation weir to irrigate the land of 221 farmers of 5 villages. Three times as much land is available for wintercropping now that there is a water supply. The farmers will probably grow vegetables and sugar as well as rice and wheat.

Population	14.6 million
Area	141,000 sq. km.
	54,440 sq. miles
Arable land	2,330,000 hectares
	5,757,000 acres
Life expectation	1960, 38 years; 1980, 44 years
Infant mortality	1960, 195 deaths;
	1980, 150 deaths
Population increase rate	2.5%
Labour force in agriculture	92%
Urbanisation	1960, 3%; 1980, 5%
Big city	Khatmandu, the capital, 255,000 people
Food index	88%
Daily Calorie supply per head	2002 calories, 89%
Basic food crops	Rice, maize, wheat, millet
Major exports	Rice
Income per head	£60
Adult literacy	About 19%
Climate	Temperate, varying with altitude

Aluko chop

Ingredients

1 large onion, finely chopped
2 level tablespoons finely chopped green pepper
1 level teaspoon salt
1½ level teaspoons turmeric
2 lb (900 grms) potatoes, boiled and mashed
about ¼ pint (1 decilitre) oil
2 eggs, lightly beaten

Makes 6 portions of 2 cakes each

Method

1. Add onion, green pepper, salt and turmeric to potatoes and mix thoroughly.
2. Cool mixture until it can be handled easily.
3. Shape into 12 even-sized round cakes.
4. Heat oil in a 12'' (30 cm) frying pan to 380°F (144°C) or to sizzling point when food is placed in it. Do not let oil smoke.
5. Using a fork, dip each cake into beaten egg and cover completely.
6. Allow surplus egg to drain, then place cakes in the hot oil and cook until brown on each side. Cakes will have a light crispy crust.
7. Lift each cake out with a spatula and drain on absorbent paper.
8. Cook remaining potato cakes, adding a little extra oil if required.
9. To keep the cakes warm after they are fried, place on a baking sheet in a very moderate oven (350°F. Gas Mark 3). Serve hot with entrée.

Source: 'Cookbook of the United Nations' by
       Barbara Kraus

Paneu

Tomato and pea dish

Ingredients

8 oz (224 grms) tomatoes
8 oz (224 grms) peas
2 onions
2 cloves garlic
1 tablespoon peeled, chopped fresh root ginger
½ teaspoon salt
Oil for frying (mustard oil is used in Nepal)
½ teaspoon turmeric
a little fresh mint
¼ teaspoon fenugreek
⅓ teaspoon ginger powder
⅓ teaspoon crushed cloves
⅓ teaspoon cummin seed
¼ cup fresh coriander leaves, chopped
1 chilli (people who do not like food hot may
   prefer to omit this)

2 servings

Method

1. Chop onion, garlic and root ginger finely.
2. Heat oil till the oil smokes a bluish colour.
3. Put first the onion, then the garlic and finally, the ginger into the oil, and cook till translucent.
4. Add spices, and cook till they smell as if they are properly done.
5. Add tomatoes, peas and chillies and cook for 15 minutes. You may need to add a little water.
6. Put in coriander leaves and mix well.

Shirley Ardener

PACIFIC ISLANDS

Fiji

(comprises about 800 islands many of them
uninhabited)

Population	630,000
Area	18,272 sq. km., 7054 sq. miles
Arable land	236,000 hectares 583,000 acres
Life expectation	1960, 64 years; 1980, 72 years
Infant mortality	1980, 37 deaths
Population increase rate	(1970/9) 2%
Labour force in agriculture	39%
Urbanisation	1980, 42%
Big city	Suva, the capital, 66,000
Daily calorie supply per head	99%
Basic food crops	Rice, taro, cassava, yams, breadfruit
Major export	Sugar
Income per head	£787
Adult literacy	75%
Climate	Tropical

Food self-sufficiency has never been a problem in traditional societies in the South Pacific. Only the influence of modern tinned food has to some extent upset the traditional balance and caused nutritional deficiencies in isolated instances where people live in urban areas. Every individual Fijian living in a village has access to farming land, and there is plenty of food for everyone. But the exploitation of copper could upset the ecological balance in the main island of the group.

An Oxfam-supported project in the South Pacific

On 1st/2nd March 1983, Hurricane Oscar hit and devastated a wide area of the Western and Southern coast of Fiji. Other outlying islands were also hit. The Salvation Army appealed to Oxfam for help to pay for five construction teams of 10 people and for food, a generator, 3-ton truck, tools and power tools. Oxfam gave £5000 to the Salvation Army towards this work.

Kokoda

Ingredients

750 grms or 1 ½ lbs fish fillets *or*
    half this quantity fish and half of shelled and
    headed prawns
Salt
1 cup lemon juice or lime juice
Chopped green onion or tomato to garnish

For the coconut sauce

2 grated coconuts
2 small chopped onions
2 medium sliced lemons with the skin on
1-4 small chillies, chopped *or* 2 teaspoons crushed
    peeled ginger root and ½ teaspoon turmeric
2 teaspoons salt
Six servings

Method

1. Cut fish fillets into 1 cm (half inch) pieces.
2. Sprinkle with salt and leave for a few minutes.
3. Pour over the fish one cup of lemon juice, or just enough to cover the fish.
4. Leave for 2-3 hours or overnight in the fridge, until the fish is white. The time taken will depend on the type of fish, the acidity of the lemon or lime juice and the temperature.
5. Strain off the juice and squeeze out moisture by pressing in strainer.
6. Prepare coconut sauce by putting together all the ingredients in a bowl and blending very well.
7. Leave the coconut sauce ingredients for about 30 minutes, then squeeze out the cream and strain.
8. Pour the sauce over the fish and garnish.
9. Serve well chilled but not so cold that the coconut sauce becomes hard.

Source:'Pacific Islands Cookbook' by Susan Parkinson and
    Peggy Stacy

Fish baked in soy sauce and ginger

Ingredients

Whole fish (e.g. cod) weighing 1-1 ½ kg (2-3 lb)
Oil
2 teaspoons fresh crushed peeled ginger
1 crushed peeled clove garlic
Up to ¼ cup soy sauce
Water
2-3 teaspoons sugar
1 tablespoon sugar
1 tablespoon cornflour
2-3 tablespoons chopped spring onions
Five or six servings

Method

1. Scale, wash and dry fish.
2. Rub it with oil and lay in a shallow pan.
3. Prepare ginger and garlic and thoroughly mix with soy sauce, ¼ cup of oil and ⅓ cup of water. Use a blender if possible.
4. Pour this mixture over fish.
5. Bake fish in oven at 180°C (350°F), basting with sauce frequently, until the fish is soft.
6. Just before serving, pour off gravy, sprinkle fish with 2-3 teaspoons sugar and put under the grill.
7. Cook until sugar has formed a shiny glaze.
8. Put fish on a serving plate.
9. Mix 1 tablespoon cornflour with ¼ cup of water. Add 1 cup of pan gravy and bring to the boil.
10. Stir in 2-3 tablespoons chopped spring onions.
11. Pour over fish and serve with rice.
Note: It may be necessary to add more water to pan gravy to make 1 cup.

Source: 'Pacific Islands Cookbook' by Susan Parkinson and
Peggy Stacy published by Pacific Publications.

Note: It may be necessary to add more water to pan gravy
    to make 1 cup.

Peru

Population	17.4 million
Area	1,285,000 sq. km.
	496,138 sq. miles
Arable land	3,400,000 hectares
	8,401,000 acres
Life expectation	1960, 47 years; 1980, 58 years
Infant mortality	1960, 163 deaths;
	1980, 88 deaths
Population increase rate	2.6%
Labour force in agriculture	36%
Urbanisation	1960, 46%; 1980, 67%
Big city	Lima, the capital, 3.8 mn.
Food index	83%
Daily calorie supply per head	2274 calories, 98%
Basic food crops	Potatoes, barley, maize, wheat
Main exports	Copper, fishmeal, zinc, silver
Income per head	£395
Adult literacy	About 80%
Climate	Temperate on coast, tropical in jungles, cool in highlands

Many Third World countries have resources which they sell to earn foreign exchange. Peru's coastal waters are very rich in fish and the port of Chimbote has an output of 150,000 tons of fish a year. The fish (sardines, mackerel, tuna and pilchards) is canned for use by humans and cats in the U.K. and other relatively rich countries, or is turned into fishmeal for animal feed. Only 0.6% of the fish is eaten in Chimbote and only 20% in Peru. As many as 70% of Chimbote's children under five years of age may be malnourished, and most of the people in Chimbote cannot afford to buy the fish that they produce. Working conditions in the canning factories are very bad indeed. The atmosphere is always cold and damp and the women are often wading in ankle-deep water and fish waste with little in the way of protective clothing.

Most of the workers in the canning factories are casual — taken on for short periods under contract by the employers, who are almost all Peruvian enterprises packing for sale to foreign companies.

An Oxfam-supported project in Peru

"The ill-health and malnutrition of the child population of Pamplona Alta is the gravest problem", writes Hilary Creed, a British nutritionist working in one of Lima's slum communities, which has between 50,000 and 70,000 people. People flock into the city from rural areas in the hope of finding well-paid employment and a better life in the capital. But the city is already crowded, and, around a central core of affluence and traffic jams, the newcomers are obliged to erect a ring of shanty housing on waste ground — makeshift shacks usually without the services of water, drainage, electricity or rubbish collection. In these conditions, their existence is bleak, and disease is rife. The children are the most vulnerable people.

In 1974, Oxfam agreed to start supporting a child Nutrition Rehabilitation Unit as part of a clinic in Pamplona Alta. But severe financial pressure forced the clinic and the Unit to close after 1½ years.

In early 1977 a modified health programme was started: Hilary Creed developed a new programme in the light of her earlier experiences. She decided to develop a programme in which she and her team would be working at the level of blocks (groups of houses) making primary health care and nutrition knowledge readily accessible. The scheme depends on health promoters who are "highly motivated youngish women with children of their own who have emerged as the health leaders for their own and neighbouring blocks. They have learned the basics of health and nutrition care and are able to impart their knowledge in a sympathetic, simple and comprehensive fashion". The health promoters work with a small professional team including Hilary Creed, Sister Mary Kenneth, the co-ordinator, doctors and nurses. Behind the promoters and the team are four health delegates who represent the communities involved.

Hilary Creed commented: "The health promoters and delegates will need continual support from us … technical medical assistance will always be needed … but the major part of the responsibility and the organisation of the programme will be theirs".

Shrimp chowder

Ingredients
2 tablespoons oil
1 clove garlic, ground
1 onion, finely chopped
1 large tomato, chopped
4 cups boiling water
1 cob of maize, cut in pieces
$\frac{1}{4}$ cup peas
1 lb. (450 grms) potatoes
2 tablespoons rice
1 lb. (450 grms) fresh shrimps, cleaned
Pinch of oregano
4 slices fried white fish
Salt and pepper to taste
1 cup evaporated milk
Chopped parsley
1 poached egg per person (optional)

6–8 servings

Method
1. Heat oil in saucepan and fry the garlic, onion and tomato.
2. Add the water, corn, peas, potatoes and rice and boil for about 10 minutes.
3. When the potatoes are cooked, remove them from the heat and add the shrimps, oregano, salt and pepper.
4. Simmer till the shrimps are cooked.
5. Just before serving, add the milk and fried fish. Sprinkle with parsley. Poached eggs can be served on top if desired.

Source: 'Cookbook' Recipes collected by the American Women's Literary Club of Lima, Peru.

Anticuchos   (Meat dish)

Ingredients

I beef heart or the equivalent weight (3½ lbs or 1575 grms) in chicken liver
2 cloves garlic, ground
¼ cup chilli sauce or
½ cup chopped hot peppers
2 cups vinegar or enough to cover the meat
½ teaspoon cumin seed
1 teaspoon salt
½ teaspoon pepper

Sauce

¼ cup ground hot peppers (chilli)
½ cup oil
3 tablespoons vinegar
2 tablespoons of the marinade

6–10 servings

Method

Note: 4-8 oz (100-200 grms) grilling meat should be enough for one portion.

1. Clean the heart or livers thoroughly (removing the nerves and the fat for instance).
2. Cut into small pieces.
3. In a bowl put the garlic, hot peppers, vinegar, cummin seed, salt and pepper and mix well.
4. Marinade meat in this sauce over night.
5. If necessary, add more vinegar so that the meat is completely covered.
6. Place the pieces of heart or liver on wooden or metal skewers and cook on a spit or rack over direct heat basting with the following sauce, till cooked.
   Prepare the sauce: Fry the hot peppers in oil, add vinegar and the marinade.

Source: 'Cookbook'. Recipes collected by the American Women's Literary Club, Lima, Peru.

Arroz tapado

Ingredients

2 tablespoons oil
2 cloves garlic, ground
Salt to taste
3 cups water
2 cups rice, rinsed in water
2 tablespoons fat
¼ cup chopped onion
2 small tomatoes, chopped
1 cup mince
¼ teaspoon pepper
½ cup seedless raisins
2 hardboiled eggs, sliced
1 tablespoon chopped parsley
Grated Parmesan cheese (optional)

Method

1. Heat the oil in a saucepan and brown half the garlic with a little salt.
2. Add water and, when it boils, add the rice. Cook slowly.
3. Fry the onion quickly with the remaining garlic and tomatoes in the fat.
4. Add the meat, salt and pepper.
5. When the meat is done, add the raisins, eggs and parsley.
6. Grease a mould or bowl and put a layer of rice, then a layer of meat mixture and lastly another layer of rice.
7. Turn out on platter to serve. Sprinkle with grated cheese, if desired.

Source: 'Cookbook'. Recipes collected by the American Women's Literary Club of Lima, Peru.

Lima beans and bacon

Ingredients

1 cup dried Lima beans or baby butter beans
4 strips bacon
1 small onion, sliced
½ cup carrots, cut in cubes
1¼ teaspoons salt
1/8 teaspoon pepper
1 cup water
6 servings

Method

1. Wash the beans, cover with cold water and let stand overnight.
2. Then drain off the water.
3. In a frying pan, brown the bacon, onion and carrots.
4. Put the beans, bacon, onion, carrots, seasonings and one cup of water in baking dish.
5. Cover and bake at 275°F (Gas mark ¼ - ½) for 3 hours.
6. Serve hot.

Source: 'Cookbook'. Recipes collected by the American Women's Literary Club of Lima, Peru.

Papas à la Huancaina

(Potatoes, Huancaina style)

Ingredients

10 potatoes, cooked and peeled.

Sauce

2 cups fresh cheese
3 hard-boiled egg yolks
2 tablespoons ground chillies
Salt and pepper to taste
1 cup oil
½ cup evaporated milk
Few drops of lemon juice
¼ cup onions, finely chopped and rinsed in boiling water
5 hardboiled eggs, sliced
10 ripe olives
1 chilli, cut into strips
Lettuce leaves.

Method

1. Arrange the potatoes on a serving dish and cover with the following sauce:
2. Mash together the cheese and egg yolks with a fork.
3. Add the chillies, salt and pepper and mix well.
4. Pour in oil a little at a time; add evaporated milk and lemon juice.
5. Beat well and lastly add onion.
6. Cover potatoes with the sauce and garnish with remaining ingredients.

Source: 'Cookbook'.

Somalia

Some parts of Somalia are natural desert, extensive additional areas have become desert or semi-desert within the last hundred years. A parched, mainly treeless landscape, with a very low percentage of arable land. Somalia has no known mineral deposits although oil exploration in its northern region is under way. There is little agriculture and almost no industry. 60% of the people are nomads.

A major part of Somalia's population is under-nourished. Water is scarce: only about 18% of the rural population has access to safe drinking water.

Population	3.9 million
Area	638,000 sq. km.
	246,330 sq. miles
Arable land	1,066,000 hectares
	2,634,000 acres
Life expectation	1960, 36 years; 1980, 44 years
Infant mortality	1960, 175 deaths;
	1980, 146 deaths
Population increase rate	2.3%
Labour force in agriculture	79%
Urbanisation	1960, 17%; 1980, 30%
Big city	Mogadishu, the capital
	400,000 people
Food index	84%
Daily calorie supply per head	2033 calories, 88%
Basic food crops	Maize, sorghum
Major exports	Bananas, hides, skins, myrrh
Income per head	Not known
Adult literacy	About 60%
Climate	Hot and dry

Oxfam-supported project in Somalia

Galka'yo town in Mudugh region lies in a plain which is dry and seemingly barren. The demand for firewood and overgrazing have together caused an area of at least 10 kms in all directions to be stripped of vegetation.

The work of the National Range Agency in Mudugh region covers sand fixation, the creation of range land reserves, the establishment of tree nurseries and shelter belts, and generally fighting desertification.

In 1982 the Agency asked Oxfam to help improve a tree nursery at Galka'yo which supplies seedlings for their activities in the region and also to individuals wishing to plant trees in Galka'yo itself. The nursery also serves as a training centre and an example to other nursery activities in the region.

The water source, which has only dried up once recently, forms a natural reservoir.

Oxfam gave £4,750 for a solar irrigation pump so that the tree nursery would get a sustained water supply, small trees and fencing wire.

Spiced tea

Ingredients

3 pints (1.6 litre) cold water
Half cinnamon stick
8 whole cardamom pods
6 cloves
2 peppercorns
Half inch (about 1.5 cm) peeled and grated fresh
    root ginger *or*
1 teaspoon powdered ginger
½ teaspoon nutmeg
Half cup sugar
Pinch tea

Method

1. Grind together the cinnamon stick, cardamom seeds, cloves and peppercorns.
2. Simmer these spices, the ginger and nutmeg gently in the water.
3. When the water is boiling, gradually add the sugar and simmer.
4. Take off the stove and add the tea. Cover and allow to stand for five minutes.
5. Pour the liquid through a strainer into a teapot or thermos flask.

Source: Melodie Winch

Seafood stew

Ingredients

1 cup onions, finely chopped
1 teaspoon curry powder
1 teaspoon ginger powder
1 teaspoon salt
1 teaspoon red pepper, crushed
¼ cup peanut oil or peanut butter
1 lb (450 grms) tomatoes, cut in small wedges
2 lbs (900 grms) seafood (for instance, cockles, mussels, shrimps, prawns). *
8 servings

Method

1. In a large saucepan heat oil and fry onions, curry powder, ginger, salt, and crushed red pepper till onions are soft.
2. Add the tomatoes, and simmer until tomatoes begin to cook.
3. Add the seafood and fry lightly for 10 minutes.
4. Serve over hot rice.

Source: "The African Cookbook", by Bea Sandler.

*In Somalia, crabmeat is used.

Competition for land between black people and
white people began very soon after the arrival
of whites in South Africa in the 17th century.
Whites forced African peasants to seek other
sources of income than farming by restricting
African agriculture to limited areas which were
often less fertile.

Now the 4.5m white people own 86.3% of the land and
21m black South Africans own only 13.7% of
the land. Average earnings in 1980 were, for
whites, R682, blacks R167.*

Since 1980 about 3m people have been forcibly
resettled on "black" land as part of the government's
"separate development" policy, leading to dis-
integration of families, land exhaustion, massive
pauperisation and severe malnutrition among
black people. Meanwhile white-owned industry
is investing in highly capital-intensive technologies
that eliminate jobs.

*R1.8 = £1.00 (1980)

An Oxfam-supported project in South Africa
In 1975, Church Agricultural Projects bought
7000 acres (2800 hectares) of dry undeveloped
and eroded land suitable mainly for ranching,
called Mdukutshani. The government had
removed all the people living there and the CAP
aimed to rehabilitate the farm, and show how to
work eroded land while training local people.

CAP is working in extremely difficult conditions,
with 22,000 people who were moved from their
previous homes, where many of them had plenty
of land and cattle. These people had had to sell
all their animals at knockdown prices and been
reduced to poverty, farming smallholdings.

The second group with which CAP is working
is migrant workers forced to return to their
"homes" in the countryside where they have little
land and no cash income.

Oxfam has been helping CAP since 1978 with
support for smallholder families with no cash
income, wages and running costs for farming
co-operatives, welfare and humanitarian relief
as well as an experimental education project for
very poor rural children.

Population	29.3 million
Area	1,221,000 sq. km.
	471,428 sq. miles
Arable land	13,572,000 hectares
	33,536,412 acres
Life expectation	1960, 53 years; 1980, 61 years
Infant mortality	1960, 135 deaths;
	1980, 96 deaths
Population increase rate	2.7%
Labour force in agriculture	28%
Urbanisation	1960, 47%; 1980, 50%
Big cities	Johannesburg 1.7 mn., Cape
	Town, 1.4 mn.,
	Durban, 997,000,
	Pretoria, 923,000
Food index	102%
Daily calorie supply per head	2831 calories, 116%
Basic food crops	Maize, wheat
Major exports	Food, gold, diamonds,
	uranium, antimony, platinum
Income per head	£978
Adult literacy	Not known
Climate	Temperate: warm and sunny

Bobotie (Curried mince)

Ingredients
$1\frac{1}{2}$ lbs (675 grms) minced beef
2 large onions
2 cloves garlic
2 slices bread
1 tablespoon curry powder
1 tablespoon vinegar
1 teaspoon turmeric
A handful of almonds
1 dessertspoonful sugar
3 eggs
$1\frac{1}{2}$ teaspoons salt
$\frac{3}{4}$ cup of milk
Use a deep, not a long shallow dish.

4–6 servings

Method
Brown the meat in oil and remove. Brown sliced onions and garlic till they are soft, which will take about ten minutes. Soak bread till it is damp in 2 tablespoonfuls of milk.
Add the onions, sugar, vinegar, salt, curry powder, turmeric and blend. Add bread and meat, and almonds, and one beaten egg. Mix well. Place in an oiled or greased casserole and pat flat. Bake in a medium oven for half an hour (say at 350 °F in an electric stove, or Gas Mark 3). Beat 2 eggs and half a cup of milk and some salt. Pour over the meat and bake for a further half hour. Get the custard brown under the grill if necessary.
Prepare Bobotie with *Cape Rice*.

Ingredients
Cup of rice
1 teaspoonful sugar
Handful of sultanas
$\frac{1}{4}$ teaspoonful turmeric
Blob of butter
2 cups water and 1 teaspoon of salt
(Rinse rice well)

3 servings

Method
Boil everything, for about twenty minutes, in a tightly closed saucepan.

Onion salad

Ingredients
6 large onions, thinly sliced
6 large tomatoes, finely cut
Salt
Lemon juice or vinegar
2 green chillies, finely chopped
2 level teaspoons sugar
Boiling water

Method
1. Rub salt well into the thinly sliced onions, in a bowl.
2. Pour boiling water into the bowl and cover onions.
3. Leave the onions in the water to stand for 5 minutes.
4. Rinse and press all the water through a colander.
5. Add finely cut tomatoes and green chillies .
6. Put the onions and tomatoes into a jar and cover with lemon juice or vinegar.
7. Add the sugar and cover the pickle.
8. Leave for one hour and serve with meat or fish.
    Rosemary Ridd.

Cape kedgeree (Fish and rice)

Ingredients:

2 oz (56 grms) butter or margarine
4 cups cooked fish, flaked
2 cups cooked rice
4 egg whites, hardboiled, chopped coarsely
2 teaspoons salt
½ teaspoon pepper
2 teaspoons curry powder (optional)
½ cup evaporated milk or light cream
4 hardboiled egg yolks, finely sieved
8 servings

Method

1. Melt the butter or margarine and add the fish. Stir gently.
2. Add the rice, the egg whites, salt, pepper, milk and curry powder if used.
3. Stir gently until thoroughly hot.
4. Garnish with egg yolks.

Source: 'The African Cookbook' by Bea Sandler

Note: This recipe originated in India where rice and moong dal (green lentils) are boiled together, perhaps with butter and caraway seeds, and given to invalids. This dish is called Kitcheree, and often served with yoghurt.

Bouba

Ingredients:

1½ oz (42 grms) butter
Handful vermicelli
1 litre (0.2 gallon) milk
Little sago
1 cinnamon stick, broken
5 cardamom seeds, peeled and stamped
Sugar to taste
Sprinkling of desiccated coconut.

Method

1. Heat the butter.
2. Add the vermicelli and fry till brown (about 5 minutes)
3. Add the milk, sago, cinnamon stick and cardamom
4. Bring to the boil, stirring.
5. Add sugar and some desiccated coconut.

Velma.

This recipe is one cooked by the Moslems in Cape Town who are in part descended from people brought from South East Asia. Bouba is drunk at the end of the day during the Moslem fast.

Pumpkin fritters

Ingredients

1½ lb (674 grms) pumpkin flesh
1 egg
4 oz (112 grms) plain white flour
¼ pint (0.14) litre milk
2 tablespoons brown sugar
2 teaspoons cinnamon powder
Salt
Pinch nutmeg
Pinch ginger powder
Sugar
Lemon juice and extra cinnamon powder to
    sprinkle on top.
Oil
4 servings

Method

1. Cut big chunks of pumpkin flesh off the skin
   (about 3 cubic inches or 9 cm).
2. Bring to the boil a large saucepanful of salted
   water and drop in the pumpkin flesh.
3. Cook the pumpkin for about five minutes till
   lumps are tender but still whole.
4. Drain away the water and leave the pieces of
   pumpkin to get cold and dry, for instance on
   kitchen paper.
5. Blend egg and flour and gradually add the
   milk to make a fairly thick batter.
6. Add the sugar, 2 teaspoons cinnamon, pinch
   salt, ginger powder and nutmeg and blend.
7. Dip pieces of dry cold pumpkin into the batter.
8. Bring to the boil a big saucepan of cooking oil.
9. Deep fry the fritters for 3-4 minutes. They
   should have a thick crisp crust.
10. Drain off the oil carefully. Sprinkle the fritters
    with cinnamon, lemon juice (and sugar if
    desired).
11. Serve as a sweet.

   Sandra Burman.

Pickled fish

Ingredients

A large fish that can be pickled:*
Plain flour
Oil for frying
1 large onion
About 1 bottle vinegar and ¼ bottle water
1 spoon brown sugar
3 bay leaves
1 chilli, chopped
2 or 3 cloves garlic, peeled, and crushed
¼ '' (1 cm) ginger root, peeled and grated
Salt to taste
¼ teaspoon turmeric
1½ tablespoons curry powder

Method

1. Clean the fish and cut into pieces.
2. Cover with plain flour and fry lightly.
3. Cut up onions and place in a saucepan.
4. Add enough vinegar to the onions to cover
   (one bottle vinegar and ¼ bottle water
   perhaps).
5. Add sugar, bay leaves, chilli, garlic, ginger,
   salt, turmeric and curry powder.
6. Allow all ingredients to boil but let the onions
   remain crisp.
7. Put the fish and onions in layers in a dish
   and place in a fridge.

Source: Rosemary Ridd, who was given the recipe by
        Christians within the Cape Town Black Community.

*Herring for example. In Cape Town yellowtail or coppeljoe
 are used.

Sri Lanka

During the 1960s, Sri Lanka developed a 'welfare state', but by the middle 1970s
these welfare programmes were absoɪbing more than a third of the country's budget, and still over a million people (many of them well-educated and qualified) were unemployed.

Since 1978, the government has reduced subsidies sharply and opened up the economy to more foreign investment and private enterprise.

There are serious communal problems between the Sinhalese majority and the Tamil minority: communal issues are closely interwoven with the fear of economic deprivation. When unemployment is high, communal tension rises.

Any development of Sri Lanka's economy at home will depend to a great extent on her foreign trade. But Sri Lanka is a classic example of a one-crop economy, being dependent on the fortunes of tea from estates established by the British on land they acquired very cheaply in the last century.

An Oxfam-supported project

The Brown Planthopper has become the major rice pest in rice-producing countries of Asia. Since 1977 this pest has attacked lowland rice crops in epidemic numbers in Indonesia, Malaysia, the Philippines, Thailand, as well as Sri Lanka and other countries. Up to 1979, the pest had caused an estimated US $300m worth of rice crop losses.

Oxfam has given about £4000 since 1976 to the Agricultural Development Centre in Kandy, a Jesuit organisation, to pay allowances for research assistants, equipment and a four-wheeled vehicle to support the research work of an entomologist working to combat the Brown Planthopper.

Population	14.7 million
Area	66,000 sq. km., 25,482 sq. miles
Arable land	2,147,000 hectares 5,305,237 acres
Life expectation	1960, 62 years; 1980, 66 years
Infant mortality	1960, 71 deaths; 1980, 44 deaths
Population increase rate	1.6%
Labour force in agriculture	53%
Urbanisation	1960, 18%; 1980, 27%
Big city	Colombo, the capital, 1.6 mn.
Food index	121%
Daily calorie supply per head	2126 calories, 97%
Basic food crops	Rice
Major exports	Industrial exports, tea, rubber
Income per head	£114
Adult literacy	About 85%
Climate	Tropical

Soojee halwa

Ingredients

3 oz (84 grms) sugar
5 oz (140 grms) water
1 oz (28 grms) milk
Good pinch powdered Spanish saffron
1 oz (28 grms) ghee
3 oz (84 grms) fine semolina
½ tablespoon sultanas
½ tablespoon slivered almonds
¼ teaspoon ground cardamom
Few extra slivered almonds to decorate

6 servings

Method

1. Put sugar, water, milk and saffron into a small saucepan and bring to the boil, stirring to dissolve the sugar.
2. In a large saucepan melt the ghee, add semolina, and fry over a low heat, stirring constantly, until the mixture is golden.
3. Add the syrup, sultanas, almonds and cardamom and cook over medium heat, stirring with a wooden spoon.
4. When the mixture thickens and leaves the sides of the pan, pour it into a buttered dish.
5. Leave till the Halwa is cold. Then cut it into diamond shapes and decorate with the almonds.
6. Serve warm or cold, with or without cream.

Source: S. Puvanachandran.

Onion Sambol

Ingredients

1 large onion
1 medium sized cucumber
1 medium sized green pepper, seeded
Juice of half a lemon
½ level teaspoon salt
½ level teaspoon pepper
3 hard-boiled eggs

6 small servings

Method

1. Slice the onion, cucumber and green pepper finely.
2. Combine in a bowl.
3. Add lemon juice, salt and pepper. Mix lightly.
4. Cut eggs in half.
5. Arrange on onion and cucumber mixture.
6. Chill.
7. Serve as an accompaniment to curry and rice.

Source: 'The Cookbook of the United Nations' by Barbara Kraus

Fish curry

Ingredients

1 lb fish roe
2 small onions, sliced
1 sliced tomato
2 teaspoons chilli powder
½ teaspoon salt
2 teaspoons lime juice
1 tablespoon oil
¼ cup coconut milk

4 servings

Method

1. Fry onions, chilli powder and tomato for five minutes.
2. Add fish and salt.
3. Simmer for 10 minutes adding coconut milk.
4. Lastly add lime juice.

Note: You can make coconut milk by adding 2 oz (56 grms) of creamed or desiccated coconut to ¼ pint (1 decilitre) hot water and stirring until the coconut is melted and you have the right consistency.

Source: Pam Ranasinghe

Population	18.7 million
Area	2,506,000 sq. km.
	967,566 sq. miles
Arable land	12,417,000 hectares
	30,682,407 acres
Life expectation	1960, 40 years; 1980, 46 years
Infant mortality	1960, 168 deaths;
	1980, 124 deaths
Population increase rate	3%
Labour force in agriculture	76%
Urbanisation	1960, 10%; 1980, 25%
Big city	Khartoum, the capital, 334,000
Food index	102%
Daily calorie supply per head	2184 calories, 96%
Basic food crops	Sorghum, millet
Major export	Cotton
Income per head	£174
Adult literacy	About 20%
Climate	Tropical. Dry in the north

The Sudan could be the granary for Africa and the Arab world but much of the farming land is unused. The waters of the Nile are relatively unexploited as well. Large quantities of food are imported. Overgrazing, erosion and the indiscriminate use of fire have led to vegetation zones disappearing, forests diminishing and the desert expanding.

Oxfam-supported projects in the Sudan

Oxfam's recent work in the Sudan has mostly been with refugees, but it is hoped that a new office will shortly be opened, making possible more intensive long-term development work.

Ful-Sudani (Peanut macaroons)

Ingredients

6 ozs (168 grms) sugar
4 ozs (112 grms) peanuts
1 egg white
½ teaspoon salt
½ teaspoon vanilla essence

Method

1. Shell the nuts and brown them.
2. Mince through the coarsest mincer of your machine, twice over.
3. Add the sugar to the beaten egg white and stir in the nuts.
4. Put on rice paper in small rocky heaps and brown in a slow oven.
5. Cool and store in a tin.

This recipe can be made fairly easily by small children.

Source: Pot Luck

Salata ma jibna

(Salad with Parmesan cheese)

Ingredients

1 cup onions, cut in thin slices
1 cup cabbage, cut in thin slices
½ cup carrots, cut in very thin slices
1 cup tomatoes, cut in ½" (1 cm) dice.
¼ cup olive oil
¼ cup lemon juice
2 tablespoons white vinegar
1 teaspoon salt
¼ teaspoon coarse black pepper
1 clove garlic, mashed
¼ cup grated cheese (eg. Parmesan) over salad

8 small salads

Method

1. Combine all ingredients except for the last two.
2. Sprinkle garlic and cheese on top of salad.

Source: "The African Cookbook" by Bea Sandler

Population	18.7 million
Area	945,000 sq. km.
	364,864 sq. miles
Arable land	5,160,000 hectares
	12,750,000 acres
Life expectation	1960, 42 years; 1980, 52 years
Infant mortality	1960, 152 deaths;
	1980, 103 deaths
Population increase rate	3.4%
Labour force in agriculture	80%
Urbanisation	1960, 5%; 1980, 12%
Big city	Dar es Salaam, 870,000 people
Food index	92%
Daily calorie supply per head	2063 calories, 87%
Basic food crop	Maize
Major exports	Coffee, manufactured goods, cotton
Income per head	£119
Adult literacy	About 66%
Climate	Tropical on coast, semi-temperate inland

The land in Tanzania belongs to the people and to the state. It cannot be bought and sold. People in a rural area must farm a minimum acreage, and work in communal systems. Tanzania, though, until recently self-sufficient in food, now has to import large amounts each year, while a large proportion of its exports are spent on oil imports.

An Oxfam-supported project in Tanzania

In the past, most rural families in Tanzania lived in scattered settlements, growing just enough grain to feed themselves till the next harvest. Each family stored its own grain and losses were estimated to range from 25% to 40% from mould, insects and general deterioration.

In recent years government policy has persuaded people to move into village communities of about 2,000-3,000 people, so larger village storage units become practical. Moreover some of the new varieties of grain which are specially drought — or disease-resistant need better storage since they deteriorate more quickly.

Two districts in Tabora Region in West Central Tanzania built village grain stores for individual farmers. The villagers would do all the building work and provide some materials where they could. Oxfam provided the funds for the other building materials and for their transport to the villages for 19 village grain stores. Oxfam's then Field Director for Tanzania, recommending the project, wrote "These new village stores will enable people to keep anything they don't need for their family use — either for future sale, or for future use in the village when food is short. So there is a lot of enthusiasm for them. They are a kind of insurance policy or a way of making money, depending on the weather."

Coconut bean soup

Ingredients

½ cup onions, finely chopped
½ cup green peppers, finely chopped
1 teaspoon curry powder
1 teaspoon salt
¼ teaspoon pepper
3 tablespoons margarine or butter
1 cup fresh tomato cut into ½'' or 1.5 cm pieces
2½ cups kidney beans from a tin, with liquid*
2 cups coconut milk**
3 cups water
½ cup cooked rice
Shredded coconut

These quantities make 8 cups

Method

1. Put the margarine or butter in a 3 quart
    (3.3 litre) saucepan.
2. Fry the onions, green peppers, curry powder,
    salt and pepper till the vegetables are soft but
    not brown. Add the tomatoes and simmer for
    another two minutes.
3. Then add the tender kidney beans, coconut
    milk, water and simmer gently for 10 minutes.
4. Add the rice.
5. Correct the seasonings to taste and serve the
    soup with a teaspoon of shredded coconut on
    each portion.

Source: 'The African Cookbook', by Bea Sandler.

Note: In Tanzania, as in other African countries,
soups and sauces are served very thick. Coconut
bean soup would be used there as a meatless
main dish by increasing the quantities of beans
and rice.

*   If you use fresh kidney beans you must soak
    them over night, rinse them in fresh water,
    and cook in more fresh water till really tender.
** See Sri Lanka for one easy way of making
    coconut milk. A more traditional way is under
    Kenya.

Spinach with groundnuts

Ingredients

16 oz (500 grms) spinach
1 large tomato
1 large onion
4 oz (120 grms) groundnuts, finely chopped
1 teaspoon turmeric
1-2 chillies
½ pint (0.25 litre) water or vegetable stock
Salt to taste
2-3 cloves garlic

Method

1. Blanch tomatoes in hot water, peel and chop.
2. Peel and finely slice onions, chillies and garlic.
3. Put onions, tomatoes and flavourings in a pan
    and cook covered at low heat with a little
    water or stock.
4. Remove stalks from spinach, wash thoroughly
    under running water, if possible.
5. Mix the groundnuts with the water or stock.
6. Add to cooking onions and tomatoes and
    continue to simmer.
7. Blanch spinach in boiling water for ten
    seconds.
8. Remove and chop finely on a board.
9. Add the spinach to the cooking mixture and
    continue to simmer for another 5-10 minutes.
10. Serve hot as a vegetable sauce.

Source: ''Tanzania Cookbook'', by Eva Sarakikya.

Chicken curry

Ingredients

1 chicken
1 clove garlic
6 cloves
2 broken cinnamon sticks
16 caraway seeds
1 large chopped onion
1-2 inch (3-6 cm) peeled and grated ginger root
3½ teaspoons Bolst mild curry powder
Large squeeze lemon
Lots of mango chutney
1 pint (0.56 litre) chicken stock
1 dessertspoon creamed coconut
Half tin baby apple
3 dessertspoons flour
1 baby tin tomato purée
2 dessertspoons oil

Method

(Cook this dish the day before you want to eat it)

1. Fry the onion in hot oil.
2. Add the garlic and cook till both are tender.
3. Add all other ingredients gradually.
4. Bring to boil, either in a pressure cooker or in a saucepan, and cook till the chicken is done. (In a pressure cooker this takes about half an hour.)
5. Remove the bones from the chicken.
6. Heat up the curry and eat it at least one day after cooking it as the spices will improve their flavour with repeated cooking.

Source: Sally Thomas

Avocado apricot jelly

Ingredients

1 medium ripe avocado
Several slices tinned apricot
1 packet jelly, any flavour
½ pint (0.25 litres) hot water
½ pint (0.25 litre) cold water

Method

1. Wash and peel the avocado pear.
2. Cut into thin rings around the seed.
3. Arrange the rings in the serving dish and leave one for decoration.
4. Place apricot slices inside the rings and around the sides.
5. Empty the contents of the packet of jelly into the measuring jug.
6. Add hot water and stir until the jelly is dissolved.
7. Add cold water.
8. Pour the jelly immediately over the fruits and cool them first in a bowl with cold water and ice cubes. Then put in refrigerator to set.

Source: "Tanzania Cookbook", by Eva Sarakikya

Fish croquettes

Ingredients

1 lb (about 450 grms) cooked fish
  eg. left over halibut, flounder, haddock, canned
  tuna or salmon
2 lightly beaten eggs
1 teaspoon salt
1 pinch saffron or a knifepoint of the saffron
  colouring called Kesari rang dissolved in water
1 tablespoon vinegar
½ teaspoon crushed red pepper
1 pinch cummin seed
3-4 tablespoons breadcrumbs plus one cup
  breadcrumbs
3 oz (84 grms) butter or margarine
2 lemon slices per guest
2 or 3 cloves per guest

Makes 26 croquettes

Method

1. Mash the fish coarsely in a 1 quart (1 litre)
   bowl.
2. Add eggs, salt, saffron or saffron colouring,
   vinegar, crushed red pepper, cummin seed
   and 3-4 tablespoons breadcrumbs.
3. Form into 2'' (6 cm) croquettes.
4. Place croquettes on a bed of the rest of the
   breadcrumbs, and press the crumbs into the
   croquettes on all sides.
5. Chill in the refrigerator for one hour.
6. Fry in butter or margarine until golden brown
   on all sides.
7. Put two croquettes per guest on a salad plate.
8. Garnish with the lemon slices studded with
   cloves.

Source: "The African Cookbook" by Bea Sandler

Maize and spinach mix

Ingredients

8 oz (240 grms) spinach
6 oz (180 grms) green maize, off the cob
2 tablespoons oil, or fat
Salt to taste

Method

1. Wash maize well till all silky threads are
   removed.
2. Cook in a little boiling salted water; you could
   also steam it.
3. Wash and cut spinach very finely.
4. When maize kernels are nearly cooked, add
   spinach and cook till the kernels and spinach
   are tender and the water considerably
   reduced.
5. Add cooking oil. Mix well and leave to cook for
   5-10 minutes.
6. Cool and serve cold with sour milk or yoghurt.

Source: "Tanzania Cookbook" by Eva Sarakikya.

Tunisia

Population	6.4 million
Area	164,000 sq. km.
	63,320 sq. miles
Arable land	4,700,000 hectares
	11,613,000 acres
Life expectation	1960, 48 years; 1980, 60 years
Infant mortality	1960, 159 deaths;
	1980, 90 deaths
Population increase rate	2.1%
Labour force in agriculture	39%
Urbanisation	1960, 36%; 1980, 52%
Big city	Tunis, the capital, 971,000
Food index	120%
Daily calorie supply per head	2674 calories, 115%
Basic food crop	Wheat
Major exports	Petroleum and petroleum products
Income per head	£557
Adult literacy	About 62%
Climate	Temperate on coast, hot and dry inland

Most of Tunisia's people live along the Mediterranean coast while the interior of the country is relatively dry and sparsely inhabited. Urbanisation is high because of rural unemployment and 400,000 Tunisians make their living in foreign countries, especially France and Libya.

Farm output represents a diminishing proportion of Gross Domestic Product (only about 17% in 1971). The Government regards the increase of agricultural production as the first national objective. Cultivation is mostly by dry farming and harvests vary greatly owing to uncertain rainfall.

An Oxfam-supported project in Tunisia

Oxfam's most recent grant was aid towards construction of a sanitary block at a girl's school at Thibar, in 1971/2.

Chakchouka (Stuffed vegetables)

Ingredients

1–3 sweet green peppers, depending on size
2 onions
8 small tomatoes
Butter or olive oil
Salt and black pepper
6 eggs
A good pinch of Cayenne pepper (optional)

3 servings

Method

1. Cut the peppers open and remove the cores and seeds. Cut them into strips.
2. Slice the onions and cut the tomatoes in half.
3. Fry the onions and peppers in butter or oil in a large frying pan.
4. Season to taste with salt, pepper, cayenne (if used) and let them stew gently in their own juices.
5. When the peppers are soft, add the halved tomatoes and continue cooking until they too are soft.
6. Taste the mixture, adding more seasoning if necessary.
7. Drop the eggs in whole, and cook until set.
8. Season again if necessary, and serve.

Source: Claudia Roden

Salata Meshwiya

Ingredients

12 oz (336 grms) firm tomatoes (skinned or unskinned)
2 large sweet peppers
1 mild onion or 6-7 spring onions, finely chopped
1 hot dried chilli pepper (optional) finely chopped
3½ oz (about 100 grm) tin tuna fish
2 hard boiled eggs, sliced
1 tablespoon capers
2 tablespoons finely chopped parsley

Dressing

1 tablespoon lemon juice
3 tablespoons olive oil
salt and black pepper

Method

1. Halve sweet peppers and grill them skin side up until they are soft and mellow.
2. Skin and seed the sweet peppers.
3. Slice off one end of the tomatoes, scoop out the seeds and juice, and slice them.
4. Cut sweet peppers into narrow ribbons.
5. Put all vegetables in a large serving dish.
6. Add tuna fish, drained and crumbled, the sliced hard boiled eggs and capers.
7. Mix dressing ingredients together, pour them over the salad and mix well.
8. Serve sprinkled with finely chopped parsley.

Source: "A Book of Middle Eastern Food" by Claudia Roden

Turkey

Population	44.9 million
Area	781,000 sq. km.
	301,500 sq. miles
Arable land	28,479,000 hectares
	70,371,000 acres
Life expectation	1960, 51 years; 1980, 62 years
Infant mortality	1960, 190 deaths
	1980, 123 deaths
Population increase rate	2.4%
Labour force in agriculture	53%
Urbanisation	1960, 30%; 1980, 47%
Big cities	Istanbul, 2,772,000;
	Ankara, the capital, 1,878,000
Food index	111%
Daily calorie supply per head	2907 calories, 116%
Basic food crops	Wheat, barley
Major exports	Fruit, vegetables, nuts
Income per head	£625
Adult literacy	About 60%
Climate	Mediterranean on the south coast, continental inland

The Anatolian plateau has sparse rainfall and little vegetation. Round the coast, the land is very fertile. Turkish agriculture is still backward with a high (usually female) labour input. Wheat yields have improved in recent years and the government has been trying to encourage the production of fruit and vegetables for export as well. There is a lot of unemployment: the economy is unable to absorb more than half the people reaching working age every year and there is widespread underemployment in agriculture and in state enterprises also.

Turkey has become a substantial exporter of labour and in 1980 there were 905,000 workers abroad, mainly in West Germany. In recent years, Turkish migrants have gone also to Libya, Saudi Arabia and Libya.

An Oxfam-supported project

Oxfam's most recent grant was in 1979/80 to help rug weavers.

Çilbir

Ingredients

6 fresh eggs
1 tablespoon vinegar
Salt
½ - ¾ pint (about 0.28-0.32 litre) yoghurt
3 tablespoons butter
1 tablespoon paprika

Method

1. Dip the eggs, still in their shells, in boiling water for a few seconds so as to set a thin layer of the white nearest the shell. This will prevent the egg white from spreading too much.
2. Break each egg into a cup and slide into another pan of boiling water to which a tablespoon of vinegar and some salt have been added. Do not poach more than 2 eggs at a time.
3. Remove the pan from the heat and leave it covered for 4 minutes.
4. Remove the eggs with a perforated spoon.
5. Arrange the poached eggs on a hot serving dish.
6. Beat the yoghurt with salt to taste and pour some over each egg.
7. Melt the butter and stir in the paprika.
8. Dribble over the yoghurt and serve.

Source: Claudia Roden

Haricot bean salad

Ingredients

4 oz (112 grms) haricot beans, soaked overnight
4 tablespoons olive oil
Juice of half a lemon, or more
Salt and black pepper
2 hard-boiled eggs
4 black olives
1 tomato, thinly sliced

Method

1. Boil the beans until very soft and tender but still firm. Don't over cook them if you are using a pressure cooker.
2. Drain the beans well.
3. While they are still hot, add the olive oil, lemon juice, salt and pepper.
4. Mix in the eggs cut in eighths, the black olives, pitted and halved, and thinly sliced tomato, taking care not to crumble or crush them or the beans.

Source: "A Book of Middle Eastern Food" by Claudia Roden

Vietnam

Population	54.2 million
Area	330,000 sq. km.
	127,413 sq. miles
Arable land	6,055,000 hectares
	14,961,000 acres
Life expectation	1960, 43 years; 1980, 63 years
Infant mortality	1960, 157 deaths;
	1980, 62 deaths
Population increase rate	2.8%
Labour force in agriculture	70%
Urbanisation	1960, 15%; 1980, 19%
Big cities	Hanoi, the capital, 1.4 mn.
	Ho Chi Minh City, 3.4 mn.
Food index	107%
Daily calorie supply per head	1801 calories, 96%
Basic food crop	Rice
Major exports	High quality rice, rubber, seafood products
Income per head	Not known
Adult literacy	About 87%
Climate	Tropical

94

Vietnam was under French colonial domination and exploitation from the mid-nineteenth century to 1954. It was under even more intensely exploitative Japanese occupation from 1940 to 1945, fought a vicious and draining war of independence from 1946 to 1954, soon again a devastating war from 1961 to 1975, and has had a number of disrupting military involvements since then. The result of a century or so of exploitation, capped by its recent environmental holocaust, is that Vietnam today stands among the poorest and least economically developed nations in the world. Its renewable natural resource base has been devastated, its infrastructure severely disrupted, and its overall economy shattered. In Northern Vietnam, the ownership of agricultural land has been collectivised since the 1940s with agricultural production carried out by co-operatives. Since 1980, various incentive schemes have been set up, subcontracting sections of co-operative land to individual families for rice production and allowing the private cultivation of fruit and vegetables on disused co-operative land. The co-op. still owns the land but does not organise the farming on individual plots except perhaps for field preparation such as ploughing and irrigation, when tractors and irrigation facilities are shared between co-operative members.

In Southern Vietnam, however, efforts to collectivise land ownership since the end of the war in 1975 have as yet failed. Almost all farming is done privately again.

An Oxfam-supported project in Vietnam
In August 1981, the people living in and around Hanoi still did not have enough vegetables to eat. Oxfam gave 1 million Belgian francs (£14,700) to a project designed to fill this gap. Each of the agricultural co-operatives in the area around Hanoi has land connected to an Institute for selecting seeds just outside Hanoi where seeds are produced for use by each co-operative. Oxfam's money would help the Institute more efficiently to select and improve seeds so that the co-operatives could improve their productivity. This would bring them extra income and also help them to provide basic fruit and vegetables to the population in and around Hanoi.

The rest of the 8 million Belgian francs needed for the project would be paid by the Belgian government and Oxfam of Belgium.

Rolls without meat

Ingredients for stuffing

1 big onion, finely chopped
⅓ cup dried mushrooms, soaked for 10 minutes
  in water, and then chopped
1 cup Chinese vermicelli, cut to ½'' (1.5 cm)
  lengths
2 medium carrots, finely chopped
1 big sweet potato, finely chopped
2 medium eggs
1 teaspoon salt

Special equipment needed

10 pieces rice paper, 12'' or 30 cm diameter.
Divide into equal quarters.

Method for stuffing

Mix all ingredients in a big bowl.

Ingredients for mixture for damping rice paper

1 teaspoon sugar
1 cup of water
1 tablespoon of vinegar

Method

1. Damp the rice papers with a cloth which has
   been dipped in the above mixture.
2. Put 2 tablespoons of stuffing in each quarter
   of rice paper, and wrap.
3. Fry in hot, deep fat for 5-8 minutes.
4. Drain cooked rolls on paper towels.

The rolls can be eaten on their own or with
lettuce, together with fish sauce.

Ingredients for fish sauce

1 tablespoon fresh lemon juice
2 tablespoons vinegar
1 teaspoon chopped hot red pepper
1 tablespoon sugar
3 tablespoons water
3 tablespoons fish sauce (from a Chinese
  supermarket)
3 cloves garlic, crushed

Source: Mrs. K. Davis

Rice with peanuts and coconut

Ingredients

½ lb (225 grms) sticky rice
½ teaspoon salt
½ lb (225 grms) peanuts (unroasted)
1 cup coconut milk, made out of 2 oz (56 grms)
  coconut cream or desiccated coconut and
  about ¼ pint (1 decilitre) hot water

Method

1. Wash the rice and rinse well.
2. Shell the peanuts. Boil them in salt water for
   8 minutes. Peel off the brown skins.
3. Make coconut milk:
   Dissolve the coconut in the hot water. Add
   more or less water according to taste.
4. Mix the peanuts with the rice. Add salt and
   coconut milk.
5. Also add boiling water up to half an inch above
   the level of the rice.
6. Boil for 3 minutes.
7. Cook over very low heat with lid on for
   30 minutes.

6 servings.

Source: Mrs. K. Davis

Vietnamese egg crêpes

Ingredients

4 medium sized eggs, well beaten
⅓ cup Chinese vermicelli, cut into ½'' (1½ cm)
  lengths
5 mushrooms, finely chopped
⅓ cup onions, finely chopped
1 big tomato cut into pieces
1 teaspoon salt
Ground black pepper
Fresh parsley, finely chopped

Method

1. Mix all ingredients
2. Fry in hot shallow fat
3. Turn once
4. Cut into slices when you serve

Source: Mrs. K. Davis

COASTAL WEST AFRICA

Nigeria

Population	84.7 million
Area	924,000 sq. km.
	356,756 sq. miles
Arable land	30,385,000 hectares
	75,081,335 acres
Life expectation	1960, 39 years; 1980, 49 years
Infant mortality	1960, 183 deaths:
	1980, 135 deaths
Population increase rate	2.5%
Labour force in agriculture	52%
Urbanisation	1960, 13%; 1980, 20%
Big city	Lagos, the capital, 3.5 mn.
Food index	87%
Daily calorie supply per head	1951 calories, 83%
Basic food crops	Yams, cassava, sorghum, millet, maize
Major export	Petroleum
Income per head	£429
Adult literacy	About 30%
Climate	Tropical

Nigeria is one of the richest countries in Africa, but its substantial revenues from oil have not been spent on projects that would be of benefit to poor people. In recent years, low oil prices and oil production have sabotaged development plans and been a cause of Nigeria's becoming indebted to the world banking system.

Ecologically, eastern Nigeria has suffered badly. The area has some of the most spectacular examples of soil erosion and "bad land" topography to be seen in West Africa. Continuous cropping has undermined the soil's fertility.

An Oxfam-supported project in Coastal West Africa

Oxfam has not worked in Nigeria since the Civil War. An Oxfam Field Office has just been opened in Senegal.

In 1982, Oxfam paid £682 to cover the cost of supplies, travel and subsistence so that 36 people could attend a 2-day seminar in Senegal. The seminar was on crop protection of the most important vegetables cultivated in this area. It looked at the problems and dangers associated with the use of the best-known pesticides and the alternatives to their use, with a view to reducing dependence on imported chemicals.

An important aim of the project was to promote exchanges between local associations and in particular to encourage their identification of their needs for training and information. The organisers hoped that then the local associations would be able to organise themselves. If the associations do not possess all the necessary skills and experience to organise themselves, they can now call on external agencies to supply additional resources.

Abala: Savoury rice pudding

Ingredients

10 oz (280 grms) rice flour
1 ground onion
2 large ground hot red peppers
¼ pint (1 decilitre) palmoil or a little less
Boiling water
Salt to taste
Banana or plantain leaves or
aluminium foil

Method

1. Put the rice flour into a bowl and add some of the boiling water gradually, stirring all the time.
2. Add ground ingredients and palm oil.
3. Stir well, add salt to taste and more water, if necessary, to make a soft dropping consistency, but not too soft or the pudding will not keep its shape when turned out.
4. Cut banana or plantain leaves into squares, discarding the midribs. Heat the pieces over a smokeless fire to make them pliable. Grease leaves or foil with palm oil.
5. Wrap spoonfuls of the mixture in the greased leaves or foil and steam for 2 hours in a steamer with a platform, OR put in a well greased pudding basin and steam for 2 hours. Use palm oil for greasing basin. For extra flavour and food value add shrimps, chopped meat, flaked fish or garden eggs to the mixture before putting it into steam.

Source: Alberta Wright

Mango banana sundae

Ingredients

1 mango, preferably fresh, but if necessary tinned
2 bananas
2 tablespoons lemon juice
½ cup pineapple or orange juice
Vanilla ice cream

Method

1. Peel the mango if it is fresh and chop it finely.
2. Peel the bananas and chop them finely.
3. Mix the mango and the bananas.
4. Add to this mixture the lemon juice and the pineapple or orange juice.
5. Place 1 scoop vanilla ice cream in a sundae dish or sherbet glass.
6. Pour 3-4 tablespoons of the mango and banana sauce over the ice cream, and serve.

Source: "The African Cookbook" by Bea Sandler

NOTE:
Mangoes are expensive in Britain but not necessarily so in Africa, Asia or Latin America. For a special occasion or if good fresh mangoes are not available we recommend a tin of Kisan mangoes from a shop run by someone from the Indian subcontinent.

Joloff rice

Ingredients

2 packets rice, washed
1 chicken
1-2 lbs (450-900 grms) steak, mutton or other meat
1 pig's trotter
8 oz (225 grms) salt beef
8 oz (225 grms) salt pork
3 small tins tomato purée or a little more
1 lb (450 grms) fresh tomatoes
4-6 large onions
Spring onions
Parsley or okra (ladies' fingers) to garnish
1 to 1½ bottle groundnut oil

Method

1. Cut up and soak salt beef, pork and trotter long enough to get rid of the salt and make them palatable. It is best to leave them overnight.
2. Cut up the other meat into small pieces.
3. Heat the oil till it is hot, and while it is heating add a slice of onion.
4. When the onion is brown, the oil is ready, and you should remove the onion.
5. Turn some of the oil into a container to be added to the rice later on.
6. Use the rest of the oil to fry the small pieces of chicken and meat. Also fry the salt beef, pork and trotters. When they are all brown, remove and keep covered in a dish.
7. Fry the onions.
8. Add fresh tomatoes, spring onions, pepper and salt and about half a tin of tomato purée.
9. Cook for a bit and then add some water.
10. Add fried chicken and cook till the gravy is as you want it.
11. Remove chicken, some of the meat, some trotters and some gravy and put in a separate saucepan.
12. To what is left add 2 tins of tomato purée diluted with enough water to cook the rice.
13. Allow to boil and then put in rice.
14. Stir and leave to boil for about 15 minutes. Then lower heat and cook slowly.
    If rice is not as red as is wanted, dilute some more tomato purée and add to the rice.
15. Stir from time to time and add some of the oil which has previously been turned out.
16. Cook till the rice is done.
17. Decorate the rice with chicken and gravy. Garnish with parsley or fried/steamed okra.

Source: Alberta Wright

Pineapple nut bread

Ingredients

2½ cups wholemeal flour
1 cup bran
1 teaspoon baking powder
1 teaspoon bicarbonate of soda
1 teaspoon salt
½ cup chopped roasted peanuts or walnuts
2 eggs, lightly beaten
¾ cup crushed pineapple, drained

Yield: One ten inch (30 cm) loaf.

Method

1. Combine flour, bran, baking powder, soda, salt and nuts.
2. Add the pineapple and the eggs and stir thoroughly.
3. Bake at 350°F (Mark 3) in greased loaf pan for 1 hour.
4. Serve thinly sliced, with cream cheese, the day after it has been cooked.

Source: "The African Cookbook" by Bea Sandler

Groundnut stew

Ingredients

6 onions
4 tomatoes
½ lb (225 grms) meat
6 smoked fish
6 okroes (ladies' fingers)
6 aubergines
Groundnut oil
3 pints (1.5 litre) cold water
3 cups ground groundnuts (peanut butter will do)
1 teaspoon chilli powder
Salt
Stock

6 servings

Method

1. Prepare and cut up the onions, meat and fish into small pieces.
2. Heat the groundnut oil.
3. Put in the oil, onions, tomatoes, meat, and fish.
4. Add the okroes and aubergines, and pour in the cold water.
5. Mix the groundnuts or peanut butter with some stock and add to the mixture. Add the red pepper and salt.
6. Simmer for half an hour.
7. Serve with rice.

Source: Mrs. Leonie Acquah

Population	28.3 million
Area	2,345,000 sq. km.
	905,404 sq. miles
Arable land	6,314,000 hectares
	15,601,000 acres
Life expectation	1960, 40 years; 1980, 47 years
Infant mortality	1960, 150 deaths;
	1980, 112 deaths
Population increase rate	2.7%
Labour force in agriculture	73%
Urbanisation	1960, 16%; 1980, 34%
Big city	Kinshasa, the capital
Food index	88%
Daily calorie supply per head	2271 calories, 102%
Basic food crop	Cassava
Major exports	Cobalt, coffee, copper
Income per head	£93
Adult literacy	About 58%
Climate	Tropical

Agriculture in Zaire has in the past suffered continuous neglect in favour of mining and industry, which usually account for about two-thirds of all exports. The Copper Belt located in Zambia extends into the Southern part of Shaba (ex-Katanga) where several minerals are extracted. The other important mining area is Southern Kasai where 90% of the world's small industrial diamonds come from.

Subsistence cultivation supplies 70% of the population of Zaire with a living, but accounts for only half of agriculture's total contribution to Gross National Product. Since the early 1970's the rural areas have not met the demands of the towns and food has had to be imported. Drought in the area known as Bas Zaire in 1978/9 led to a famine among part of the rural population and a severe shortage of staple foods in Kinshasa. The overwhelming majority of the rural people in the country are poor and underfed.

An Oxfam-supported project in Zaire

Malnutrition is a continuing problem for the people of Bandundu province in Central Zaire. Their staple crop, cassava (or manioc) contains very little protein. Insects and caterpillars provide some animal protein, but insufficient for good health. The poor sandy soil in much of the area is not suitable for the good cultivation of other crops, although maize, millet and some rice and groundnuts are grown.

The Belgian Congo Government, before independence, launched a massive campaign to introduce fish farming throughout the country. Over 70,000 fish ponds were established in Bandundu province alone. Some were poorly constructed, often a long way from villages, and others failed as a result of low productivity, for little vegetation grew in the ponds to feed the fish. But the main cause of failure was the lack of local involvement.

In 1973, Oxfam helped initiate a survey by an American Peace Corps fisheries expert to look at the possibility of reviving small scale fish farming. Following his favourable report, the Peace Corps drew up a programme to introduce a number of their volunteers trained in fisheries to work with villages in several provinces. Work started in 1975 and by 1977 there were 13 Peace Corps Volunteers at work, and a further 7 were recruited by the end of 1978.

The programme was designed so that little is required from outside the fish farmers' own villages. And once they have learned the basic methods of fish production, they have no further need of technical assistance or outside support.

Once farmers have expressed interest in fish farming, they have to 'contribute' several months of labour for each pond they put into production. They bear all the costs themselves, but there is no charge for the services and advice of the Peace Corps Volunteer.

Between 1975 and 1978 Oxfam provided funds totalling £10,715 for transport for the volunteers (small motorcycles), materials and tools to build fish ponds, publications, and funds for establishing fish farmers' co-operatives. Support for the project has continued.

Meat and bacon dish

Ingredients

3 or 4 sweet potatoes
7-8 tomatoes, cut up
3 big onions
2 stalks parsley, chopped
18 ozs (about 500 grms) minced meat
6-8 ozs (about 150-200 grms) bacon cut into slices
2 cups rice
Salt
Pepper or red chilli powder
Water

Method

1. Wash and sieve the rice and boil it in 5 cups salted water.
2. Peel and boil the sweet potatoes in salted water.
3. Cut up the bacon and fry it in a small frying pan.
4. Peel and cut up the onions in pieces.
5. Remove the bacon and brown the onions in the bacon fat.
6. Put in the parsley and the tomatoes.
7. Add the minced meat and the pieces of cooked sweet potato. Add the bacon and seasoning.
8. Add half a cup water if the dish is too dry.
9. Put alternate layers of cooked rice and the meat and vegetable mixture into a greased dish and serve hot.

Source: ''La bonne cuisine congolaise''

Rissoles of peanuts and potatoes

Ingredients

1 cup of boiled potatoes
2 dessertspoons milk
½ dessertspoon butter or margarine
2 teaspoons flour
2 soup spoons finely ground peanuts
1 egg
Hot red pepper powder
Salt

Method

1. Mash the potatoes, and add salt and pepper powder.
2. Melt the fat in a frying pan and mix in the flour.
   Add the milk and stir till the sauce is thick.
3. Add the potatoes and peanuts, while stirring well.
4. Turn the mixture out onto a plate and divide into balls.
5. Roll the balls in lightly whipped egg white.
6. Then roll them in slightly salted breadcrumbs.
7. Fry in very hot oil until the rissoles are golden.

Source: ''La bonne cuisine congolaise''

Zambia

Copper production dominates the country. The rural areas of the north and centre are short of manpower because in the past many men went to work and live in the Copper Belt.

The government's policy is to boost hybrid maize production, which has benefited commercial farmers (both white and black) at the cost of peasant producers. Much of the best land is owned by commercial farmers.

Many peasant farmers are not in a position to take advantage of government inducements to grow hybrid maize, which is the main means for rural people to earn money for their cash needs.

An Oxfam-supported project in Zambia

The Tonga people who live in the remote and neglected Gwembe Valley were forcibly removed from the fertile Zambesi river plain when the Kariba Dam was built. They now live on marginal land which cannot support them.

In 1981/2 the rainfall in the Gwembe Valley was half the usual amount. The food crops failed completely: even the sorghum crop withered. Because of the drought the Tonga were reduced to selling their animals in order to raise cash to buy maize flour. Maize flour was not available in this area at government-controlled prices and local traders took advantage of this fact to sell the flour at twice the normal price.

The Ibwe Munyama Mission, after requests from groups of local people, started bringing in maize flour which would be sold at a price which covered purchase and transport costs only. As a relief measure Oxfam gave £6,146 as a revolving interest-free loan to pay for maize flour. The money would be repaid after the next harvest.

The project was a success, the people were fed and the traders had to drop their prices.

Population	5.8 million
Area	753,000 sq. km.
	290,700 sq. miles
Arable land	5,108,000 hectares
	12,621,800 acres
Life expectation	1960, 40 years; 1980, 49 years
Infant mortality	1960, 151 deaths;
	1980, 106 deaths
Population increase rate	3.1%
Labour force in agriculture	65%
Urbanisation	1960, 23%; 1980, 43%
Big city	Lusaka, the capital, 599,000
Food index	95%
Daily calorie supply per head	2002 calories, 90%
Basic food crop	Maize
Major export	Copper
Income per head	£238
Adult literacy	44%
Climate	Tropical

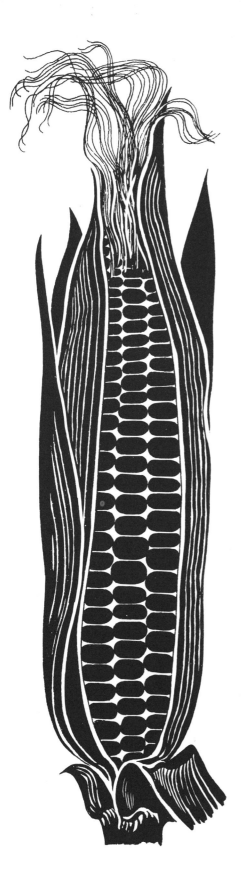

Polenta pie (Meat and maize pie)

Ingredients
1 cup maize flour
1 cup leftover chicken or other meat
1 cup thick white sauce or gravy
2 tablespoons margarine
Salt and pepper to taste
4 cups milk or 2 cups milk and 2 cups water
(preferably stock)

4 servings

Method
1. Set the oven at a medium heat (3-4 Gas, or 350°F).
2. In a small pan, make the white sauce or gravy.
3. Use one cupful of milk and thicken it with one spoonful of flour.
4. Mix the dry flour with a little cold water, and then add it to the boiling milk.
5. Put the four cups of milk into another pan with salt and pepper, and bring it to the boil.
6. Cook over a medium heat until it becomes thick, then add the margarine and stir until it is dissolved.
7. Rub the inside of an oven dish or baking tin with oil or fat.
8. Line the bottom and sides of the oven dish or tin with the maize dough, keeping back about one quarter of the dough for the top.
9. Mix together the roughly chopped meat with the sauce or gravy, and season well with salt and pepper.
10. Pour this into the prepared oven dish or tin.
11. Cover with the remaining maize dough, pressing the edges together carefully.
12. Bake in a medium hot oven for about three quarters of an hour until the pie is nicely brown.

Source: 'Home Cooking, Part I'. Compiled by the Women's Section of Zambia Broadcasting Services, with the Department of Community Development, and published by NECZAM, Lusaka.

Zimbabwe

Population	7.4 million
Area	391,000 sq. km.
	150,900 sq. miles
Arable land	2,539,000 hectares
	6,273,800 acres
Life expectation	1960, 49 years; 1980, 55 years
Infant mortality	1960, 118 deaths;
	1980, 74 deaths
Population increase rate	3.3%
Labour force in agriculture	58%
Urbanisation	1960, 13%; 1980, 23%
Big city	Harare, 686,000
Food index	97%
Daily calorie supply per head	2576 calories, 109%
Basic food crop	Maize
Major exports	Tobacco, gold
Income per head	£268
Adult literacy	About 74%
Climate	Subtropical

The first government of Zimbabwe, elected on universal adult suffrage, came to power in 1980 after a long and bitter war of liberation.

For many years, under white rule, half the land was available for white people to farm and the black majority, which outnumbered the ruling group many times over, was allocated the less fertile half, much of it far from railway lines and markets.

By 1982, more than 800,000 black families were crowded onto the 40 million acres where Africans are allowed to farm, and there is acute land hunger.

While the number of white farmers did drop after independence, there has been very little penetration by Africans into the commercial farming sector. The new government's plan to resettle African families on either unfarmed land or land bought from whites has made little progress.

Zimbabwe is a leading member of the Southern African Development Co-ordination Conference, whose objective is to ease economic ties to South Africa. But the new country is no less dependent on its powerful neighbour than it was at the time of independence. The direct and indirect threat from South Africa must be regarded as the most serious threat to Zimbabwe's stability.

An Oxfam-supported project in Zimbabwe

A recent national disability survey showed that most of Zimbabwe's 276,000 disabled people live in the rural areas and have no access to any kind of rehabilitation services or physiotherapy. Most funds for the disabled are channelled through institutions, which care for only about 2% of the affected population. The National Council of Disabled Persons of Zimbabwe was set up in 1975 by a group of disabled people based in a black township in Bulawayo to provide for the needs and welfare of the disabled through pressure on government and public education; and to encourage activity among the disabled themselves.

In 1980 Oxfam gave them funds for knitting and sewing machines to set up a knitting cooperative, for some orthopaedic devices and towards office expenses. In June 1981 Oxfam agreed to fund the Director's salary for a year. He himself is a disabled person. The NCDP has now decided to expand its present activities of establishing groups of home-based disabled people, with the aim of identifying as many rural disabled people as possible; assessing their needs for rehabilitation and ensuring they receive proper treatment; introducing, teaching and demonstrating horti-culture and agriculture as therapy in rehabilitation, and as vocational training leading to useful occupations; and fostering and encouraging the co-operative spirit among disabled people. Up to 1983, Oxfam had given £17,799 to the NCDP.

Roast pumpkin

Ingredients

1 pumpkin
1 or 2 onions
1 teacup cold water
2 dessertspoons fat
2 dessertspoons flour
Salt
Small pieces of meat (optional)

Method

1. Skin and cut up pumpkin into square blocks.
2. Heat fat.
3. Skin, slice and fry onions in the fat.
4. Add the pumpkin, cover, and cook in the fat until the pumpkin turns brown.
5. Remove the onion and pumpkin.
6. Stir in the flour with the browned fat, and cook for a few minutes until it is brown.
7. Add the water. Boil it.
8. Add salt, pumpkin, meat (if used) and onions, and heat again.
9. Serve hot.

Note
This dish will taste best if you cook it in a thick pot in ashes. But you can use a frying pan instead.

Source: "How to cook for your family" by D. Cartwright and C. Robertson

Bean soup

Ingredients

1 teacup beans (not red kidney beans)
1 onion
2 dessertspoons fat
Bones
4 teacups cold water
Salt
2 dessertspoons flour
Half or one teacup milk

4-5 servings

Method

1. Soak the beans overnight. Take off the skins. Heat the fat.
2. Skin and slice the onion. Fry it in the fat until it is turning brown.
3. Add the beans, water, salt and bones. Boil for 2-3 hours (or less in a pressure cooker) until the beans are soft.
4. Remove bones.
5. Beat to mash the beans well.
6. Stir milk into the flour. Add the soup and boil for 10 minutes.

Source: "How to cook for your family" by D. Cartwright and C. Robertson

Passionfruit cream

Ingredients

17½ oz packet (about 210 grms) orange jelly
1½ cups boiling water
2 cups passion fruit juice*
1 cup heavy cream
Toasted desiccated coconut

This makes one quart (1.3 litres)

Method

1. Dissolve the jelly in the boiling water.
2. Add the passion fruit juice.
3. Chill until the mixture begins to set.
4. Stir well.
5. Whip the cream until it is stiff.
6. Fold the cream into the partially stiffened jelly.
7. Pile into wine glasses.
8. Decorate with a mound of toasted coconut in the middle of each dessert.

Source: "The African Cookbook" by Bea Sandler

*Passion fruit juice may be bought in speciality shops. If it is not available, use apricot nectar.

Green mealie fritters

Ingredients

6 cobs of very green maize (or sweetcorn if absolutely necessary)
1 egg, beaten
Salt
6 dessertspoons flour
2 dessertspoons fat
Chopped onion   )
Chopped parsley) optional

Method

1. Remove maize from the cob. Pound well.
2. Mix the maize, salt and egg.
3. Stir in the flour until the mixture is thick.
4. Heat the fat. Fry the mixture in small cakes.
5. Serve hot.

NOTE
The amount of flour would depend on how green the corn (mealie) cobs are. The green ones make the best fritters.

Source: "How to cook for your family" and "Pot Luck"

Notes for teachers of Home Economics

Cooking is an art in which we show our sensitivity to other people's needs and customs. The UK is a multi-ethnic society, and cooking offers an excellent opportunity to learn more about the majority and minority groups which comprise our nation.

In fact our diet already includes many foods and recipes from overseas. Few countries import more of their foods than the UK! We are already extremely fortunate in having many restaurants serving relatively cheap and nutritious dishes from other continents.

In a multi-ethnic society, it is a courtesy and a responsibility to learn to eat and cook dishes from many different communities. It is also an acknowledgment to school students from ethnic minorities that their ways of life are respected. Failure to include reference to the diets of these groups and to offer a choice of foods to cook in Home Economics classes is tantamount to saying that they are unimportant and implies their inferiority. In these circumstances it is not surprising that majority group students come to regard them as such.

For this reason we think that all school canteens should regularly include dishes from communities other than majority groups. Exam syllabuses should reflect the fact that we now live in a multi-ethnic society.

It has been found that when new dishes from overseas have been cooked in schools, students from majority groups have learnt to appreciate the food more readily and are likely to be more tolerant of cultural diversities.

When we cook for people with whose eating habits we are unfamiliar, it is important to find out what our guests like to eat and to plan accordingly. Some books in the bibliography should help you in this exploration.

Home Economics teachers may be in charge of classes with students who have special food requirements because of their religious or cultural background. We ask teachers to respect the requirements. These beliefs have deep historical roots and we should recognise the importance of diet in affirming personal identity.

But diet and cooking methods change when people move and alter their way of life and cooking equipment, and as the availability and cost of foods dictates. It may be appropriate therefore to suggest additional or alternative foods to those normally chosen which are consistent with the student's religious or cultural beliefs.

This situation offers a great opportunity to Home Economics teachers who also have the chance to advise students from minority groups to avoid bad habits that may have developed in our own society.

You will be aware, for example, that when recipes require frying it is preferable to use a vegetable oil rather than butter or ghee, which is commonly used for cooking in the Indian subcontinent. But you could advise your students to avoid using coconut oil, which has a very high percentage of saturated fatty acid. Soya bean oil is best to brown food quickly and groundnut oil is best for long slow cooking. Fried foods should be drained carefully. You could also warn your students about the health hazards of eating too much salt and too much sugar.

Many people in minority groups in the UK today feel themselves to be under severe social and economic pressure because of unemployment, low pay, poor living and working conditions. These factors may affect their health.

For example, Vitamin D deficiency is more common among some minority groups than among the host community. And although most Asians from the Indian subcontinent undergo an examination to check that they are free from tuberculosis soon after their arrival in the UK, there is a high incidence of TB among the Asians from the subcontinent settled in this country.

Many British black people feel that an improved environment and the elimination of poverty are prerequisites to good health and much more of a priority than a change of diet or food supplements.

Some notes on diets eaten by minority groups in the UK

1. Indian subcontinent (India, Pakistan and Bangladesh)

A wide variety of diets is eaten in the subcontinent. A detailed appreciative description is available free from Oxfam Education Department.

Many Hindus from the subcontinent are lacto-vegetarians and, as well as refusing fish and meat, prefer not to eat eggs. But veganism is almost unknown in the subcontinent. Probably the most appropriate contribution that the Home Economics teacher can make is to recommend lacto-vegetarian students to increase their consumption of milk, yoghurt, curds and buttermilk (all very culturally acceptable) and cheese (not as common in India as in the UK). You may find it appropriate to show lacto-vegetarian students how to supplement their diet with Tofu soybean curd and miso soybean purée, which may be new to students from the subcontinent. You could also point out that familiar foods such as nuts, especially almonds, and dried fruit like dates, sultanas and apricots are also rich in iron. You could encourage your lacto-vegetarian students to eat more spinach, carrots, coriander leaves, green leafy vegetables and dark vegetables of any kind.

Gujaratis from India, and Bengalis from both West Bengal in India and Bangladesh are used to eating a diet rich in vegetables. But Panjabis from India and Pakistanis are not accustomed to do so. You may be able to show students from both these areas how to add particularly nutritious vegetables to their diet.

2. Muslim diet. The preferred diet of Muslims, both from the subcontinent and from elsewhere, is the same as that of Jews who eat only kosher food, about which much has been written. The most important restrictions are that the meat of the pig is not eaten, and animals have to be killed by a particular method. See, for more information, ''A taste of heaven'' (in bibliography).

3. Chinese diet From a nutritional point of view the Chinese diet as cooked at home is good because generally it is low in fat, high in fibre and rapidly cooked.

4. Rastafarian diet The Mosaic laws form the basis of the Rastafarian diet. No food derived from pig may be eaten. Some Rastafarians are vegans and may be vulnerable to Vitamin B12 deficiency anaemias. You could show Rastafarians how to extend their diet, as in the section for lacto-vegetarians from the Indian subcontinent. Other Rastafarians feel able to eat milk or eggs. Most Rastafarians prefer not to eat salt unless it is seasalt, and refuse processed foods. The diet is usually rich in fibre.

Portrait of a Home Economics classroom

Christine Traxon, Head of Home Economics at Holyhead School, Birmingham, writes ''I try to build an environment where the children (pupils) feel perfectly secure in sharing information about how things are done in their own homes. If I'm aiming to teach about fish, for example, I want it to come up quite naturally what fish they eat at home and how it is prepared.

So instead of announcing 'Next week we are going to do Jamaican food', I find it better to introduce one basic food element as a theme and then discuss the different forms it can appear in.

If we're taking beans, for example, I'd mention black-eyed beans, and seeing my familiarity with something they know, the children pour in examples of other varieties they know about.

… If I'm not familiar with some children's home customs, I can unwittingly cause offence — and the children will clam up … Once we were playing a game where the pupils had to name vegetables, using different letters of the alphabet. It came to B and they said 'Bananas'. If one doesn't know, or forgets, that bananas *are* a vegetable for some West Indians, it's very easy to say 'Of course, they're not vegetables'. It's a matter of how you phrase a question so that you find out from them.

'What made you say bananas?' could lead to a discussion about the differences between vegetables and fruit.

After four years' teaching, I am still finding out new things — for example, that it is against the religion of some to eat certain things at certain times…''

This extract is from ''Multicultural education'' by John Twitchin and Clare Demuth, published by the BBC.

Teachers are free to reproduce material from this book for use in their own schools.

Making culinary analyses of recipes

The recipes included in this booklet are the results of centuries of development. They illustrate that, all over the world, food has been regarded as a source of pleasure as well as a means of satisfying hunger and helping to maintain health. The recipes can thus be read not only as instructions for making specific dishes but as sources of ideas for different ways to combine, cook and serve foods.

In order to do this, recipes must be analysed from a culinary point of view — ie, by asking what is the culinary function of each ingredient in the recipe. Does the ingredient provide flavour, bulk, moisture, crispness, binding for other ingredients or does it combine with other foods to provide a mixture with distinct properties? Analysing recipes in this way can be a fascinating hobby which builds up a respect for the ingenuity and imagination shown by cooks all over the world throughout the centuries. An indication of this ingenuity can perhaps be seen by looking at the ways in which cooks use just two foods.

Wheat and rice are both cereals which can be ground to produce white powders which contain starch. However, the wheat flour so produced also contains gluten, whereas rice flour does not, and without the gluten it is not possible to produce the elastic dough needed for making bread, cakes and pastries. Nevertheless cooks in both rice- and wheat-growing areas have ways to satisfy many common culinary needs. The solutions cannot be exactly the same, not only because of the chemical differences, but also because of factors such as costs, time, facilities and traditions. The following table merely hints at how the process of making culinary analyses of recipes may be started: —

Some culinary uses of wheat and rice		
Solutions		
Need	**Wheat**	**Rice**
Thickening liquids:—		
adding solids	pasta added to soups and stews	rice grains added to soups etc.
using thickening agents	wheat flour blended with cold water, or mixed with fat to form a roux, then boiled	rice flour blended with cold water and then boiled with the main liquid
absorbing liquid	pasta can do this if used in sufficient quantity as in macaroni pudding	ground rice or rice grains used in stews and puddings
Bulk in a meal	pasta, pastry and bread; cakes and biscuits	steamed, boiled or fried rice; compressed rice squares or balls
Neutral base	bread and pastries; pasta when served mixed with other foods	cooked rice to which other foods are added
Wrappers and covers	patties	dried rice papers (Vietnamese)
FUN	long spaghetti	rice noodles and vermicelli

NB
In wheat-growing areas, other cereals and root vegetables often serve the same functions as rice in recipes because people find it more economical to reserve the wheat for making bread.

Marjorie Cay

SAFFRON

SOYA BEAN

OREGANO

VANILLA

TURMERIC

PEANUTS

SWEET PEPPER

SESAME

SWEET POTATOES

YAM

TARRAGON

PEPPERCORN

109

Glossary

Allspice – A small tropical tree whose unripe berries provide the spice called allspice because it combines the flavour of several spices.

Aubergine – (known also as egg plant). A vegetable native to tropical Asia, widely grown in tropical, subtropical and warm temperate regions for its purple fruit.

Avocado pear – A fruit native to Central America, it has now been widely planted in the tropics and a few subtropical areas. Avocado pear contains more protein than any other fruit, up to 25% of fat, much Vitamin A and B.

Cardamom – The tiny black seeds are usually marketed in their pods, and pounded, after they have been extracted, to make powder which is used as a flavouring. Cardamoms are used to prepare curries, and in confectionery. Cardamom comes originally from South-West India and Sri Lanka.

Cayenne pepper – "Red" or cayenne pepper powder is obtained from the powdered dried fruits of two kinds of chillies (see below).

Chilli (or small hot peppers)
– The chilli plant is a perennial,
When ripe, chillies are bright red and smaller than sweet peppers. They vary in pungency but in general it is greater than in the sweet pepper and some chillies are very hot indeed. Chillies often look wrinkled because they have been dried in the open air in the sun. They are essential ingredients in curry powder and are used in making pickles and tabasco sauce. India is the biggest exporter.

Chilli powder – A powder usually made of mixtures of various kinds of chillies.

Cinnamon – The cinnamon tree grows in the wild. Commercially cinnamon is available in powdered form and as sticks (which are used whole). Cinnamon comes mainly from Sri Lanka and South India.

Cloves – Cloves can be used whole or ground.

Coconut milk – You can make coconut milk by grating the flesh of a coconut into a bowl and adding one pint of boiling water; stir and set aside for 30 minutes. Then squeeze and strain the milk through muslin or fine cotton. You can also pour real milk over desiccated coconut to get the same result.

Coriander – Coriander seeds when crushed are a delicious mild spice which can be used in curries. The leaves have quite a strong flavour and are also used in cooking. The coriander plant grows in the Mediterranean area, Africa, India and Mexico.

Courgettes – French marrows. When mature, they are no different from British marrows, but they have been developed for cutting when they are only a few inches long.

Cowpeas – A pulse originating in Africa but now cultivated in many tropical areas. Cowpeas have a high protein content both in their seeds and pods.

Cumin – The whole seeds can be used as well as the ground seeds, but cumin should be gently warmed to bring out the aroma before it is put into the cooking pot or sprinkled on meat.

Fenugreek – Fenugreek is a native of the Mediterranean region. It is also cultivated in the Indian sub-continent. Its seeds have been used medicinally since ancient times. In India the seeds are used in curries.

Garlic – Garlic bulbs or heads are made up of several "cloves" within the skin of the parent bulb. Garlic should be crushed or chopped finely.

Ghee – (clarified butter). The desired cooking medium for most Indian dishes. Today most people use a vegetable ghee which is available in Indian and Pakistani grocery shops.

Ginger – Ginger is available in four forms: (1) as fresh root ginger, which you should peel and chop up very finely indeed; (2) powdered, when the root has been dried and ground; (3) as stem ginger in syrup; (4) crystallised (to be eaten as a sweet). In Indian, Chinese and Malay cookery, fresh root ginger is an important ingredient. Ginger powder is also an important ingredient when curries are being made. A small piece of stem ginger plus a little powdered ginger can be used if root ginger is unobtainable. But usually stem ginger is eaten as a dessert. The finest quality dried root ginger comes from Jamaica.

Lima beans – Lima beans originated in Peru and are popular in the U.S.A. Dried Lima beans are sold as butter beans and are available in supermarkets.

Litchis – (sometimes pronounced ly-cheese). A fruit native to China. Litchis are usually eaten fresh but they are also sometimes tinned for export or preserved in syrup. Litchi nuts can be prepared by drying the fruit, when the pulp takes on a nutty raisin-like flavour.

Lovage – A vegetable and herb garden plant used like celery as a vegetable.

Nutmeg – is the inner kernel of a fruit borne by a tree native to the Molucca islands of Indonesia, which were for centuries the great source of nutmegs. Nutmeg is generally sold in powdered form, but whole nutmegs can be bought and grated at home. The only important producing countries now are Indonesia and the island of Grenada in the eastern Caribbean.

Okras – Sometimes called ladies' fingers, this vegetable is native to tropical Africa.

Olives and olive oil – The olive tree grows wild on the shores of the Mediterranean Sea, where it has been cultivated for centuries, but it is also grown elsewhere. The olives ripen in autumn and though many are eaten fresh or preserved, the bulk of the crop is pressed for oil.

Oregano – Wild marjoram, dried.

Palm oil – The oil palm originated in West Africa where it grows wild. Unrefined palm oil is yellowish because it contains carotene from which our bodies can form Vitamin A.

Paprika pepper – The powder obtained from the ground seeds of sweet peppers (capsicum annuum) (qv). The best paprika pepper is Hungarian. N.B. Paprika powder and cayenne pepper are quite different.

Peanuts – (often called groundnuts). They originated in South America, but India and China are now the biggest producers, and Nigeria is the biggest exporter.

CINNAMON

AUBERGINE

ALLSPICE

CORIANDER

AVOCADO PEAR

CARDAMOM

CLOVES

CHICKPEA

CASSAVA

COURGETTES

CAYENNE PEPPER

CHILLI

111

Pepper – Both white and black pepper are made from grinding peppercorns which grow on a climbing vine. The peppercorns turn red when they are ripe. Pepper is a native of India and is still chiefly grown in southern Asia. India is the largest exporter. Pepper was originally used in India largely in curry powders, of which it was the most pungent ingredient until chillies were introduced from America in the sixteenth century. To obtain black pepper, unripe peppercorns are simply sun-dried. To obtain white pepper, ripe peppercorns are soaked and the outer coverings rubbed off the seed. Pepper has been historically the most important spice in world trade and exports sometimes reach 75,000 tons a year.

Saffron – Saffron consists of the dried styles of certain crocuses. It is used as a spice. Whole saffron is usually cheaper than powdered saffron. To cook rice with saffron: put the styles or the powder in the water you want to boil as you heat it. Get the water the right colour before you add the rice.

To cook sweets using saffron: put the saffron in before the mixture boils.

Saffron is the richest known natural source of riboflavin (Vitamin B2). The pigment in saffron offsets the effects of high cholesterol levels in the blood system and may have a specific action against hardening of the arteries. But saffron must not be taken in more than culinary quantities. Because of the high cost of saffron, many Indian families who would otherwise have used it now buy Kesari rang (i.e. saffron colour).

Sesame – The seeds are sprinkled in or on cakes, breads or sweetmeats, especially in the Middle East, but many families in the tropics stew the seed whole. Oil is also obtained from sesame seeds. The plant originated in Africa, but now India, China, Burma as well as the Sudan are the chief producer countries and Nigeria also exports sesame.

Soy sauce – comes from the soya bean which is very rich in protein. Note: there are at least two varieties of soy sauce, the Chinese and the Japanese. Make sure you use the right variety, or you will ruin the flavour of your dish.

Sweet pepper – (capsicum annuum). This is an annual species which originated in tropical America. When ripe the fruits (used for cooking or in salads) are red, yellow or brown, but immature fruits of the large mild kinds are often picked when still green. These peppers vary greatly in shape and pungency: some of the big ones are quite mild though the seeds are usually hot. All sweet peppers have a very high Vitamin C content. Sometimes the large mild sweet peppers grown in Europe are called "paprikas"; Spanish ones are called "pimientos".

Tamarind – The tamarind tree has pods which contain a brown pulp. This is eaten fresh and used, especially, as a souring agent. Allow 4 tablespoons hot water for 1 oz or 28 grams tamarind, unless otherwise stated. Soak the tamarind in hot water for 30 minutes; then squeeze it and strain it. Discard the pod and the seeds but use the water and pulp.

Tarragon – This herb is a native of southern Europe. If you cannot obtain fresh tarragon, buy dried French tarragon and do not keep it more than one year.

Turmeric – A root of the ginger family. It gives a yellow colour and spicy flavour to food. It is mainly grown for local consumption in India and other tropical Asian countries, and almost all exports are from India. If turmeric is not kept in an airtight container the attractive smell quickly disappears.

Vanilla – Vanilla beans are the pods of a climbing orchid native to Central America.

Yoghurt – You can make your own yoghurt cheaply by boiling a pint of cows' milk and cooling it to blood heat; take 5 teaspoons of commercial natural live cows' milk yoghurt and smear it evenly inside a bowl. Pour the milk back and forth from bowl to pan three or four times. Then cover the bowl with a clean cloth and leave undisturbed in a very warm place, without draughts, for about 8 hours or overnight, or till the yoghurt is set. Store in the refrigerator.

Specialist ingredients

Chinese, Indian sub-continent and Indonesian spices and flavourings and specialist Chinese foods are available on mail order from Ken Lo's kitchen, 14 Eccleston Street, London SW1. (Telephone: 01 730 4276/7734).

But many of the spices and flavourings required for cooking recipes are available from health food shops under their English names.

Indian, Pakistani, Bangladeshi, Chinese, Caribbean or other ethnic minority shops will sell many of the ingredients too.

GOURDSEEDS

LIMA BEAN

COWPEAS

LITCHIS

NUTMEG

GARLIC

GINGER

CUMIN

OLIVES

BULRUSH

MILLET

SORGHUM

MAIZE

OKRAS

Some spices and flavourings used in cooking from the Indian Sub-continent (The spelling is as close to the pronunciation as possible)				
English	**Hindi/Urdu**	**Panjabi**	**Bengali**	**Gujarati**
Asafoetida** x	Heeng	Hing	Heeng	Heeng
Basil*	Tullsee	Tullsee	Toolsee	Tul-see
Bay leaves	Tej paat	Tej pate	Tej pataa	Limra
Black onion seed	Kalonji	Kalo jeere	Peeaz beez	
Cardamom +	Ilaaichee	Lachee	Aylaach	Ellchee
Cayenne pepper)* Chilli powder)*	Choora mirch	Pisi mirch	Goora lanka	Bhooko marcha
Green chillies**	Hari mirch	Hari mirch	Kachha lanka/ morich	Leela marcha
Red chillies with fruit not yet dry**	Laal mirch	Laal mirch	Pakka lanka/ morich	Laal marcha
Red chillies, dry but whole**	Sukhee laal mirch	Sookee laal mirch	Shooknoo lanka / morich	Sukha marcha
Cinnamon*	Daal cheenee	Daal cheenee	Daroo cheenee	Taj bhooko
Cloves**	Lawaang	Long	Loboongo	Lawing
Coriander*	Dhania	Dhania	Dhone	Dhana
Coriander leaves*	Hara dhania	Hara dhania	Dhone pataa	Dhana patta
Cummin *	Zeera/Jeera	Zeera or Jeera	Jeere	Jeera
Fenugreek*	Methee	Me-thee	Methee	Methee
Hot mixed spices or Garam masala**	Garam masaala	Garam masaala	Gorum moshla	Garam masala
Garlic*	Lehsun	Thom	Roshun	Lasen
Ginger*	Adrak	Adrak	Adar	Aa-doo
Lovage*	Aajwine	Jowine	Jooan	Ajma
Mace*	Jaavitri	Jaavitri	Joitree	Javoontree
Mango powder ‡	Aamchoor	Amchoor	Aamchoor	Ambchur
Mint*	Pudeena	Poodna	Podina	Fudeena
Mustard seed*	Sarson	Rai	Shorshe	Rai
Nutmeg*	Jyefal	Jyefal	Jyephol	Jaifar
Black pepper**	Kaa-lee mirch	Kaa-lee mirch	Golmorich	Mari
Dried pome-granate seed	Anaardaanaa	Anaardaanaa	Shukno betana beech	
Poppy seed*	Khashkas	Khuskhas	Posto	Khaskhas
Saffron**x	Kesar	Keser	Zafraan	Kessar
Salt**	Nammak	Nammak or Loon	Noon	Neemak
Sesame*	Teel	Til	Teel	Tal
Tamarind ‡	Imlee	Imlee	Taytool	Amlee
Turmeric*	Haldee	Haldee	Hol-ood	Hardar
Yoghurt ‡	Da-hee	Dayee	Doy	Dahee

KEY   Very strong flavour**   Used in sweets +   Reduces heat in spicy dishes ‡
Milder flavour *   Gives sour flavour ‡   Use a pinch only x

114

Some vegetables and fruits used in this book				
English	**Hindi/Urdu**	**Bengali**	**Gujarati**	**Panjabi**
Aubergine or eggplant	Began	Begoon	Ringan	Bengan or Vathu
Cabbage	Band gobhee	Bandha kohpi	Kobee	Band gobi
Capsicum (see Green sweet pepper)				
Cauliflower	Fool gobhee	Full kopee	Full kobee	Full gobi
Carrot	Gajjar	Gajjar	Gajjar	Gajjar
Cucumber	Kheera		Kakree	Kheera
Green sweet pepper or Capsicum	Leela mirch	Kashmiri morich	Mora marcha	Shimla mirch
Ladies' fingers or Okra or ochroes	Bhindee	Dherosh	Bhinda	Pindee
Maize	Makka	Bhootta	Makai	Makhi (Cob-Sitta)
Mango	Aam	Aam	Keri	Amb
Onions	Pee-aaz	Peeaaj	Dungaree	Pee-aaj
Peas	Mattar	Motor shoti	Mattar	Mattar
Potatoes (or Irish potatoes)	Aa-loo	Aa-loo	Bateta	Aa-loo
Pumpkin	Kaddoo	Koomra	Kore-oh	Kaddoo
Radish	Moolee	Moola	Moora	Moolee
Spinach	Saag	Shaag	Bhaji	Saag
Sweet potato	Shakarkand	Mishti aaloo	Sakhariya	Shakkar kandee
Tomato	Tamaatar	Tameto	Tameta	Tamaata

Pronunciation Key:

a = "u" as in "hut",
oo = oo as in "woo"

u = "u" as in "butcher",
aa = "a" as in "bath"

e = é in French

Warning: Mustard seeds tend to jump so keep the lid on pan.

	Non-animal Protein Foods					
British English or Indian English	Scientific Name	Hindi/Urdu	Panjabi	Bengali	Gujarati	Caribbean
Blackgram or Urd	Phaseolus mungo	Urad	Urad Mah	Mashkalai	Arad	Woolly pyrol
Butter beans or Lima beans	Phaseolus lunatus					
Chickpeas Bengal gram or Yellow gram	Cicer arietinum	Channa or Kahboolee Channa	Cholay or Channe	Chola or Channa	Channa	Channa
Chickpea flour		Besan	Vesan	Beshan	Channa lott	
Cowpeas	Vigna unguiculata	Bora				
Groundnuts or Peanuts	Arachis hypogaea	Moongfaly	Moongfoolly	Cheena badam	Magfarree	Peanuts
Hyacinth beans or Lablab or Bonavist bean or Lubia	Dolichos lablab	Lobhia	Harwah	Noba	Waal	
Kidney (Red) beans	Phaseolus vulgaris	Raajmaa	Mothi		Poso	(Red) peas
Moong beans or Green gram	Phaseolus aureus	Moong	Moong	Kachha moog	Mag	
Pigeonpeas or Red gram	Cajanus cajan	Arhar or Too-wer	Toor	Ar-har	Tu-er	Gungo peas
Red lentils (split)	Lens culinaris (split or unsplit)	Masoor daal	Mahsoor daal	Mushuree dahl	Maasoor daal	Lentils
Soya or Soy beans	Glycine max	Soya	Soya			Soy beans
Split peas	Pisum sativum (split or unsplit)	Mattar daal (split)	Mattar daal (split)	Motordal	Mattar daal	Split peas

N.B.
In Hindi and other North Indian languages, a lentil, beans or legume when whole
is called 'gram' and when split, 'daal'.

For pictures of these foods, see "The Oxford Book of Food Plants"

Staple foods: their place of origin, their dispersal and their usefulness			
Crop	**Place of origin**	**Dispersed to:**	**Usefulness**
Rice	Asia	Africa, South America, USA, Australia, Southern Europe	With wheat, the world's most important food crop.
Wheat	probably S.W. Asia & E. Mediterranean	Asia, North and South America	The most important cereal in temperate climates
Potatoes	South America	All parts of the world except low tropical regions	Potatoes can yield higher food value per hectare than any cereal. But they have a high water content, a shorter storage life and greater wastage than cereals.
Maize (also called Indian corn, mealies; sweet corn is a sweet kind of maize grain	Americas	All parts of the world	A very important cereal crop in tropical and subtropical regions. It provides about a quarter of the world's grain requirements.
Millet (Tropical varieties)	Some varieties originated in Asia, others in Africa	Tropical areas	Very drought resistant. Millet stores well. It tolerates poor soils. Usually eaten as a porridge.
Sorghum	Africa, probably	Widely dispersed in semi-arid tropical and subtropical regions	Very drought resistant. It doesn't store well. It tolerates poor soils. Eaten as a porridge or a pancake. Very good for making beer.
Cooking bananas, sometimes called plantains	South East Asia	South America, Africa, Caribbean, etc.	Forms staple food of millions of people in East Africa. The bananas are usually steamed or roasted.
Breadfruit	Pacific Islands	Most parts of the tropics	Staple food in some Pacific Islands. Usually roasted.
Cassava (or Manioc)	Americas	Almost all parts of wet tropics	A most important food plant. Stores for 2 years in ground after reaching maturity. Main nutritional content is starch. Usually boiled and mashed.
Sweet potatoes.	South America	All over wetter tropical regions	Usually a secondary food crop. Does not store well. Usually boiled and mashed
Taro, eddo, dasheen or old cocoyam	Pacific, Caribbean, West Africa apparently	Many parts of wet tropics	A crop of secondary importance. Very fine grained, digestible starch, as in arrowroot
Tannia or yautia or new cocoyam (a relative of taro)	West Africa		
Yams	Most varieties originated in Asia or Africa	Now especially important in high rainfall zone of West Africa, and in Vietnam, Laos, Kampuchea, Caribbean and Pacific Islands	Stores better than most tropical crops. Can be boiled, mashed, roasted or fried. Nutritional content mainly starch. A staple food in parts of West Africa, it has an extremely rich social and religious history

Note (spanning Rice and Wheat usefulness): These two make up about half the world's grain requirements.

Main source: "The Oxford Book of Food Plants"

Comments on and explanation of statistics

We have added some statistics to give basic information about the countries from which the recipes come. No one statistic adequately conveys the standard of living of one country relative to another, but the statistics we have selected together do give some indication of relative standards of living.

Population and Land

The area of arable land and land under permanent crops in a particular country provides a better guide to that country's potential in relation to its population than the total area.

Most countries mentioned in this book have experienced a rise in life expectation and a drop in infant mortality rates* in recent years. Population increase rates have come down in most areas except Africa. But a country with an increase rate of 1% a year will double its population in 70 years, and in a country with a 2% annual increase rate, the population will double in 35 years. Few countries can afford a high rate of population increase, but parents are usually reluctant to have really small families (even assuming birth control is available) until they are fairly sure that some children will live to be adults.

Use of land and work on the land

Unjust land tenure systems and the political, economic and social policies which enable these systems to prevail are a major cause of hunger and poverty in the Third World today. A rural family or community with the secure use of a piece of land will almost certainly grow their own food before they consider any other crops. But the same land in the hands of a landlord, a government or a foreign firm is far more likely to be used to grow whatever is most profitable.

In some places smaller farmers are forced to sell up their land to bigger ones in times of bad harvest or illness, and so they join the ranks of the landless. The figures show the percentage of the economically active population who work in agriculture, forestry, hunting and fishing.

In many parts of the world, landowners wanting to make large profits have cut down on the traditional labour force and perhaps use labour-saving machines instead. But in most Third World countries, jobs outside farming are scarce and few people leaving the land have the right qualifications for such opportunities as are available. So in many countries, shanty towns of unemployed or underemployed migrant workers are springing up outside the main cities. The urbanisation figures show the percentage of the total population living in towns in 1960 and in 1980.

Food Index

This figure shows the food production per head of population taking a 3-year average so as to make allowance for good and bad harvests. The figure includes food exported as well as food eaten inside the country.

If the index shows 75%, that means that food production in 1978-1980 was 25% less than it was in 1969-71, which is taken as the base year.

The figure for the daily calorie supply gives the number of calories available per head of population, and we have included also the percentage which that figure represents of the requirements for human nutrition.

Income per head per year

This figure is calculated by dividing the total Gross National Product (the value of all goods and services produced per year in a particular country, plus net income from abroad) by the population of that country. This figure gives an indication of the wealth of one country compared with another, but gives no information as to how the wealth is distributed.

Literacy

This figure shows the percentage of the adult population who are literate.

Source of Statistics

Our main sources were the Food and Agriculture Organisation of the United Nations Production Year Book 1981, and the World Development Report 1982, published for the World Bank by Oxford University Press. We have also used the Commonwealth Fact Book published by the Commonwealth Secretariat in 1982. The Economist Intelligence Unit Quarterly Economic Reviews have also been a constant source of help.

Where dates are not mentioned, we have used latest available figures.

*Deaths of children aged 0-1 years per 1000 live births.

Index of basic cooking methods

Baking and breadmaking
Bolivia, Brazil, Caribbean, Central America, Chile, China, Cyprus, Lebanon, Mexico, Pacific Islands, Peru, South Africa, Sudan, West Africa, Zambia.

Boiling
Brazil, Caribbean, Central America, Chile, Cyprus, Indian subcontinent, Indonesia, Mexico, Mozambique, Peru, South Africa, Sri Lanka, Tanzania, Turkey, Vietnam, West Africa, Zaire, Zimbabwe.

Frying (deep)
Algeria, China, Indian subcontinent, South Africa, Vietnam.

Frying (shallow)
Algeria, Brazil, Burma, Caribbean, Central America, Chile, China, Cyprus, Egypt, Indian subcontinent, Indonesia, Lebanon, Malaysia, Mexico, Nepal, Peru, Somalia, South Africa, Sri Lanka, Tanzania, Tunisia, Vietnam, West Africa, Zaire, Zimbabwe.

Griddle
Central America, Kenya.

Grilling
Indonesia, Kenya, Lebanon, Mozambique, Pacific Islands, Peru, South Africa, Sudan, Tunisia.

Marinading
Caribbean, China, Indian subcontinent, Indonesia, Malaysia, Mexico, Mozambique, Pacific Islands, Peru.

Poaching
Peru, Turkey.

Roasting
China, Indian subcontinent, Mozambique.

Roux method
Central America, Indonesia, Mexico, Zaire, Zambia.

Simmering
Algeria, Brazil, Caribbean, Central America, Chile, China, Colombia, Cyprus, Egypt, Indian subcontinent, Kenya, Lebanon, Malaysia, Mexico, Morocco, Peru, Somalia, Sri Lanka, Tanzania, Vietnam, West Africa.

Steaming above boiling water
Caribbean, Indian subcontinent, Indonesia, Morocco, Tanzania, West Africa.

Steaming in a bain-marie
Indonesia

Steaming in a pressure cooker
Caribbean, Indian subcontinent, Tanzania, Turkey, Zimbabwe.

Sweetmaking
China, Mexico, Sri Lanka.

Uncooked food
Caribbean, Cyprus, Indian subcontinent, Jordan, Lebanon, Mexico, Morocco, Mozambique, Pacific Islands, South Africa, Sri Lanka, Sudan, Tanzania, Tunisia, West Africa.

Wok or quick frying
China.

Different kinds of food

AVOCADO PEARS (see vegetable dishes)

BANANAS AND OTHER STARCHY TREECROPS
Caribbean, Central America, China, Indonesia.

BEVERAGES
Somalia, South Africa.

CEREALS
Maize
Bolivia, Caribbean, Central America, Chile, Mexico, Tanzania, Zambia, Zimbabwe.
Rice
Caribbean, Indian subcontinent, Lebanon, Peru, Sri Lanka, Vietnam, West Africa.
Wheat
Chile, Indian subcontinent, Kenya, Lebanon, Mexico, Morocco, South Africa, Sri Lanka, West Africa.

EGG DISHES
Burma, Cyprus, Indonesia, Peru, Tunisia, Turkey, Vietnam.

FIBRE-RICH DISHES
Brazil, Caribbean, Central America, Indian subcontinent, Lebanon, Morocco, Peru, Tunisia, Turkey, Vietnam, West Africa.

FISH AND SEA-FOOD
Brazil, Caribbean, China, Indonesia, Kenya, Mexico, Pacific Islands, Peru, Somalia, South Africa, Sri Lanka, Tanzania, West Africa.

FRUIT DISHES
Caribbean, Central America, Malaysia, Morocco, Tanzania, West Africa, Zimbabwe.

MEAT
Chicken
Caribbean, Chile, China, Colombia, Indian subcontinent, Indonesia, Malaysia, Mozambique, Peru, Tanzania, West Africa, Zambia.
Cow
Algeria, Caribbean, Chile, China, Cyprus, Egypt, Indian subcontinent, Indonesia, Lebanon, Peru, South Africa, West Africa, Zaire.
Lamb and Sheep
Algeria, Cyprus, Egypt, Indian subcontinent, Indonesia, Lebanon.

Pig Brazil, Caribbean, Central America, China, Cyprus, Malaysia, Peru, West Africa, Zaire.

Salt
Caribbean, West Africa.

MILK AND MILK PRODUCTS
Bolivia, Brazil, Caribbean, Indian subcontinent, Jordan, Mexico, Peru, Turkey.

NUTS
Cashewnuts
Indian subcontinent.
Coconuts
Brazil, Caribbean, Tanzania, Vietnam.
Peanuts/groundnuts
Sudan, Tanzania, Vietnam, West Africa, Zaire.

POTATOES (see Root crops)

PROTEIN-RICH NON-ANIMAL FOODS
(see also Nuts)
Brazil, Caribbean, Central America, China, Indian subcontinent, Morocco, Peru, Tanzania, Turkey, Zimbabwe.

ROOT CROPS
Potatoes
Brazil, Colombia, Nepal, Peru, South Africa, Zaire.
Sweet potatoes
Caribbean, Zaire.
Yams
Caribbean.

SALADS
Caribbean, Cyprus, Lebanon, Morocco, Mozambique, South Africa, Sri Lanka, Sudan, Tunisia, Turkey.

SNACKS AND SIDE DISHES
Indian subcontinent, Indonesia, Sri Lanka.

SOUPS
Algeria, Central America, Colombia, Cyprus, Indonesia, Tanzania, Zimbabwe.

SUGAR AND SWEETS
Brazil, Central America, China, South Africa, Sri Lanka, Sudan.

VEGETABLE DISHES
Caribbean, China, Cyprus, Indian subcontinent, Kampuchea, Mozambique, Nepal, South Africa, Tanzania, Vietnam, Zimbabwe.

We are particularly grateful to the publishers of the following books for permission to use recipes:

*''Potluck'', published by the girls of Farringtons, Chislehurst, Kent.

*''The cookbook of the United Nations'', by Barbara Kraus, published by Nelson, 1967. With their help, we have tried several times to trace any present copyright holder, but without success.

*''The African cookbook'', by Bea Sandler, published by the World Publishing Co. New York and Cleveland. We have tried in vain to trace any present copyright holders.

*''Cooking the Indian way'', by Attia Hosain and Sita Pasricha, published by Lalvani Publishing House in 1967. Recipes reproduced by permission of Hamlyn Publishing Group Ltd.

''Cookbook'' of recipes collected by the American Women's Literary Club, Lima, Peru.

''Tanzania cookbook'', by Eva Sarakikya, published by Tanzania Publishing House, Dar es Salaam, 1978.

''The cooking of the Caribbean Islands'', by Linda Wolfe, published by the editors of Time-Life Books, 1977.

''La bonne cuisine congolaise''.

''Pacific Islands Cookbook'', by Susan Parkinson and Peggy Stacy, published by Pacific Publications.

''How to cook for your family'', by D. Cartwright and C. Robertson, published by Longman Group.

''Chinese food'', by Kenneth Lo, published by Penguin Books Ltd, 1972.

''Captain Blackbeard's Beef Creole'', published by Peckham Publishing Project.

''The flavour of Hong Kong''.

''The Hong Kong Cookbook'' published by Vista Productions, Ltd., Hong Kong.

*Out of print.

Bibliography On food and diet

''The Oxford book of food plants'', by G.B. Masefield, M. Wallis, S.G. Harrison, B.E. Nicholson, published by Oxford University Press, reprinted 1981.

''Asian families and their foods'' by City of Bradford Metropolitan Council Directorate of Education Services.

''Indian cooking'', by Savitri Chowdhary, published by André Deutsch, 1954.

Books by Kenneth Lo on Chinese food.

''Food in Chinese culture'', edited by K.C. Chang, published at Yale, 1977.

''A taste of heaven'', by June Rose and Lionel Blue, published by Darton, Longman and Todd. (Excellent material on people's dietary preferences). 1977.

''African cooking'', by Ola Olaore, published by W. Foulsham and Co. Ltd., at Slough, 1980.

Oxfam Education Department has published materials with plenty of background information about food and farming: —

''India: country and people'' £3.00
A village community study in India: ''Samanvaya School'' £3.90
''Jamaica: country and people'' £4.95
''Bolivia: country and people'' £3.95
''Botswana: country and people'' £2.00
A pack featuring Bangladesh: ''Looking after Ourselves'' £4.95

Please allow 20% for postage.
We also distribute free information sheets on diets of ordinary people.

On ecology and environment

''Food for beginners'', Susan George, published by Writers' and Readers' Co-operative, 1982.

''How the other half dies'', by Susan George, published by Penguin Books, 1976.

''Losing ground'', by Erik P. Eckholm, published by W.W. Norton and Co. Inc., New York.

''The New Internationalist'', available from 42 Hythe Bridge Street, Oxford.